HOW TO BE HAPPY
HOW TO BE HOLY

by

Fr. Paul O'Sullivan, O.P.
[E.D.M.]

"Pray without ceasing."
—1 Thess. 5:17

TAN BOOKS AND PUBLISHERS

CUM PERMISSU SUPERIORUM.

APPROVED BY HIS EMINENCE CARDINAL M. CEREJEIRA,
PATRIARCH OF LISBON.

ISBN: 978-0-89555-386-7

Library of Congress Catalog Card No.: 89-051901

Printed and bound in the United States of America.

TAN BOOKS AND PUBLISHERS
1989

*Read, dear friend, these pages,
and you will pray as you have
never prayed before.*

My dear Father Paul O'Sullivan,

I approve and recommend with all my heart the new book that you have just published: *How to be Happy—How to be Holy*.

The subjects you treat of are of the very highest importance and vital interest. The counsels you give are so easy and yet so useful that everyone without exception can put them into practice. They guarantee what we all so earnestly desire, namely, a happy life and the abundant blessings of Almighty God.

I sincerely hope that this book will be read not merely once, but repeatedly by all who wish to be good Christians. From its reading they will reap the greatest benefit.

I bless you, dear Father.

✝ *M., Cardinal Patriarch*,

Lisbon, November 10, 1943

CONTENTS

Introduction

READ, CATHOLICS, READ

We venture to say that very few books will give such genuine pleasure and do so much real good to their readers as this precious booklet.

Hundreds of thousands of Catholics are daily saying their morning and evening prayers without deriving the grace, strength and consolation they might so easily derive from these lovely prayers.

They learned to pray as children, and during all their lives they continue to say their prayers with the vague ideas, the imperfect understanding that they acquired as children.

They have done little to develop, to improve, to make more clear the ideas that they got in their childhood. The result is that a vast number of Christians merely repeat the words without giving any attention to the sense of what they are saying. In other words, they have not an intelligent grasp of the act they are performing.

As a consequence they get comparatively little benefit from their prayer and do not enjoy the consolation of prayer.

This booklet has in view to teach Christians:

a) How to pray.

1

b) **How to derive immense benefits from prayer.**
c) **How to enjoy the deep consolation of prayer.**

It is not necessary to be a saint to enjoy prayer. Everyone who *knows* how to pray finds intense delight in prayer.

To pray well demands no hard or difficult effort, nothing that the ordinary Christian cannot do with pleasure if only he *knows* how to do it.

First of all, what is prayer and how should we pray?

Prayer is certainly not the mere repetition of words without giving any attention to their meaning though, unfortunately, this is the way that thousands of otherwise good Christians are praying every day.

What then is prayer? Prayer is nothing else than talking to God, conversing with God Himself.

When we kneel down and make the Sign of the Cross reverently, God at once turns to us and gives us all His attention as fully as if there was no one else in existence.

Can this be true? It is absolutely true, and as a consequence, when we pray we are enjoying an intimate, personal conversation with God Almighty. What a joy! What a privilege! What an immense consolation!

We are speaking to God as truly and as really as Moses spoke to Him on Mount Sinai, as truly, as lovingly as Peter and John and Magdalen when He was on earth.

True, we do not see God with the eyes of our body, but we are perfectly sure by our faith that God is really and truly listening to every word we are saying.

Oh, if Christians would only grasp this glorious truth, what delight would they not have in prayer!

This was the secret of the Saints, but it is a secret so clear and easy that anyone can understand it.

Why did the Saints love to pray? Just because they knew and they felt that they were talking to God. Therefore, far from being wearisome it was an immense joy for them to pray.

This then is the first clear idea we must have when praying, *viz.,* that we are talking to God in the most real and true sense of that word. There is nothing clearer, easier to understand, nothing more certain.

The second great thought is that God has bound Himself most solemnly to hear our prayers.

"Ask and you shall receive, seek and you shall find, knock and it shall be opened unto you." What words could possibly be clearer? These and similar promises our Blessed Lord made over and over again.

It is quite certain that we never send up a prayer to God lovingly and confidently that He does not hear, and that does not bring us a great grace in return.

We never yet said one prayer, never yet sent up

one cry to God that was not heard. Of this there can be no possible doubt.

Sometimes God may not give us what we ask because He sees that it would not be good for us, but undoubtedly in this case He will give us another and a better grace.

This, too, is an idea that we must thoroughly understand.

A third truth which we must bear in mind is that every prayer we say with reverence and trust, such as any ordinary Christian can say, gives God immense glory and pleasure.

What a joy it should be to feel that we are giving real joy to God.

But does God really bother about us? God does not only love us, but He most earnestly desires our love and affection in return. "Behold the Heart that loves men so much, but is so little loved by men." These are His own very words addressed to each of us.

Fourthly, our prayers obtain for us many important graces and blessings which we shall never get and never enjoy if we do not ask for them.

If a Christian believes these truths, as he is bound to do, is he not a madman if he omits his prayers?

Fifthly, all men desire happiness, all men seek happiness, all men work for happiness.

Unfortunately, men seek happiness in a thousand different ways and never find it. They lose their time.

God alone gives happiness, as God alone gives life and health. Happiness is God's greatest gift, for it embraces what is best for us.

God, as we have said, promises to give us all good things if we ask for them. What can be easier than to ask God every day in our prayers for happiness?

Why do not men ask God for happiness? They do not think.

True, it is not possible to have perfect happiness in this life, because we are in a vale of tears due to the sin of Adam and due to our own sins, which bring so much sorrow and suffering with them. However we can have a great measure of happiness in this life, and it is God and God alone who can and will give us this great measure of happiness if we confidently and lovingly ask Him for it. There is no better, no surer way of attaining happiness than by praying for it. Men who do not pray for happiness must be very ignorant, or very foolish.

On the other hand, all of us have to face some suffering. No one can avoid suffering, sickness, pain and disappointments.

But here again God helps us. No pain comes to us without God's permission; not even a hair falls from our heads without His consent.

When God permits suffering He always helps us to bear it. He always gives a grace, a strength, a consolation which enables us to bear the cross He sends us. But once more, we must ask Him. The very suffering He sends is a reminder to us to go to Him, to ask His help. In pain and sorrow and danger we run to God as the little child runs to its mother in the moment of danger.

One may ask, "But do we not see men in the world happy who do not pray to God?" God allows all in His infinite mercy and compassion a certain measure of the goods of this life. He makes His sun to shine on the just and the unjust, but the pleasure, the joys, the happiness of men who do not love God are full of bitterness and sadness. Their lives are exposed to many and cruel disappointments, and in their sufferings they have no real comfort, they have no one to go to for consolation.

The good Christian knows that for every pain he has, he will have a great reward in Heaven. He knows that his sufferings are nothing else than a part in the sufferings and Passion of his Lord.

Every word and act of Our Lord was a lesson for us to learn, an example to follow. The greatest lesson of all, the greatest proof of His love for us was His suffering for us.

Who, then, is not ready to suffer a little for the love of that God who suffered so much for us?

Our Lord, who was God, suffered; His Blessed Mother suffered. All good men suffer, but they feel that they are only having a little share in the sufferings of their dear Lord. They know full well that every pain will have its reward forever in Heaven, that five minutes' suffering is worth far more to them than years of pleasure and joy.

Above all, they feel that God is helping them to suffer.

Therefore real peace and happiness God and God alone can give and gives to all who ask Him for it in prayer.

PRAYER IS THE GREATEST POWER, THE GREATEST CONSOLATION IN THE WORLD

Let us give one clear example: Solomon was the wisest of men. He enjoyed all the delights which wisdom gives. He was immensely rich; there seemed to be no limit to his wealth. He had pleasures, honors and power.

Yet he tells us that in all these pleasures he found no real happiness. It was only in God that he found happiness and joy.

Solomon is no exception, for it has become a proverb that "Uneasy is the head that wears a crown." If kings and the great ones of the earth fail to find happiness, how can other poor mortals hope to achieve it?

Finally, whatever little happiness worldlings may claim is lost in death, and they are always afraid of death. Death always has terror for them. Whereas, God's friends not only enjoy the great measure of peace, joy and happiness which God gives them, but they are sure of a still greater happiness after death for all eternity.

Death for them is not the grave, the tomb; it is

only the gate of infinite joy and bliss for ever and for ever.

Oh, Christian man, pray, pray much to the good God for happiness!

Lastly, our prayers deliver us from countless evils and dangers.

How many people, for instance, would have good health did they earnestly ask God for it? Doctors and remedies are necessary, but it is God who gives doctors and remedies the power to preserve our health or restore it to us.

Only recently an eminent American doctor, a Protestant by religion, published a striking article on the power of prayer in restoring health of mind and body. He says, "How very, very often have I not seen my patients restored to health when all my skill and the skill of my colleagues had utterly failed. Prayer—and I mean the prayer of the ordinary Christian—is the greatest power in the world." To any observant Christian, especially a doctor, this fact is manifest.

Without referring to the thousands and thousands of people miraculously cured every year at Lourdes, at Fatima in Portugal and at many other shrines, also by the intercession of St. Philomena, the Little Flower and other saints, prayer is every day obtaining from God relief from suffering and restoration to health.

We do not know what evils and dangers may lie in wait for us during the day. Therefore, let us pray.

PRAYER DELIVERS US FROM THE GREATEST EVILS

We have a striking case of the power of prayer in the history of the pious King Ezechias.

Sennacherib, the powerful ruler of Assyria, gathered together a mighty army and besieged King Ezechias in Jerusalem. There seemed to be no hope of delivery.

The King, full of faith, went to the temple and poured forth his soul in fervent prayer before God and also besought the Prophet Isaias to intercede for him. The Prophet sent him word not to fear, because God had heard his prayer and would Himself destroy the army of the Assyrians.

The same night God sent His angel to the camp of the Assyrians and slew one hundred and eighty-five thousand of the enemy.

The Assyrian King fled in terror to his country, where he was miserably slain by his own son.

Some time after this extraordinary answer to prayer King Ezechias fell gravely ill, and the Prophet Isaias announced to him on the part of God that his hour had come and that he must prepare himself.

The holy King, while thoroughly resigned to God's will, still, full of confidence prayed earnestly for some more years of life if such were pleasing to God.

Once more the Almighty showed His divine pleasure at the confidence of His servant and granted Ezechias 15 more years of life.

How many Christians would regain new life if they prayed fervently and received the last Sacraments, in time and with faith, instead of putting them off until it is too late.

Chapter 1

THE MORNING OFFERING

On rising in the morning we should drop on our knees for a moment and make the following offering to the Sacred Heart of Our Lord:

Sacred Heart of Jesus, through the pure hands of Mary I offer Thee all the prayers, works and sufferings of this day and of all my life for the intentions of Thy Sacred Heart, for the Apostleship of Prayer and for all my own intentions. (Some like to add:)

Every breath I draw this day, every beating of my heart, every step I take, every word I say, every movement of my body and mind I wish to be an act of love for Thee such as Thy Blessed Mother herself performed.

This act is short, but we should say it with full deliberation. It is of the highest importance, for it transforms every act of the day, every work, every suffering into an act of love, into an act of merit.

What thousands of acts of love we can thus perform! What immense graces we shall receive! What glory we shall give to God!

And if we do not make this short act, what thousands of graces we lose each day.

But can there be any doubt of this fact? None whatever.

St. Paul, the great Apostle of the Gentiles, tells us clearly to do everything we do in the name and for the love of Jesus Christ.

He mentions even the most ordinary and material actions of the day. He says, "Whether you eat or drink or whatever else you do, do all in the name of Our Lord, Jesus Christ."

And what can be more natural? Let us see why. It was God who made us, who gave us all our faculties, our eyes, our ears, our head, our heart.

He gave us all these faculties that we may use them to serve and love Him.

It was He who gave us those wondrous eyes that constantly offer us such visions of beauty. They bring us into contact with the sun and moon and stars. With them we see the great mountains and the vast ocean, and the green valleys, and the beautiful flowers and trees.

They, too, help us to look on the faces of our dear mother and father and friends and enjoy their sweet and loving smiles.

Do we ever thank God for those wondrous eyes? How natural and how right it is to say, "O my God, I wish that every glance of my eyes be an act of love for Thee."

Who gave us this wonderful heart that is beating, ticking every moment like a clock, for the last twenty, forty, sixty years?

It is God that keeps it beating. Should it stop for one moment, we would die.

How many countless times does this wonderfully delicate organ pump the purple blood through our bodies every day!

Do we ever thank God for this heart?

How natural, how easy, how right it is to say once and many times a day: "O dear God, I wish that every beating of my heart be an act of love and gratitude for Thee!"

And so with our other faculties we should wish to thank God for all those glorious organs that He has given us.

Do we ever thank Him for our intelligence and free will, which make us like the angels, nay like to God Himself?

How easy, how proper it would be to say frequently: "O my good God, I wish that every thought that passes through my mind be an act of love for Thee. I wish that every act of my free will be in union with Thy Divine Will."

In this way every day of our lives would be full of numberless acts of love and merit.

HOW ST. GERTRUDE EXPLAINS THIS TRUTH

St. Gertrude, to make this doctrine perfectly clear, tells us of a wicked man, full of hate for God, who on arising in the morning made this impious act: "O God, I believe in You, but I hate You with all the power of my soul. I wish that every act I do this day be an act of hate and blasphemy against You. I wish that every step I take, every word I say, every single act I do be a blasphemy against You, a blasphemy like to those that the devils in Hell are ever uttering."

Not satisfied with this diabolical act of wickedness, he repeated these words many times each day so that his every act was a blasphemy and an act of hate against God.

Now the Saint asks, why do not Christians do the contrary?

Why do they not make their Morning Offering with great deliberation? It will only need a moment. It will make their every act an act of the love of God, as truly as the acts of that wicked man were acts of diabolical hate.

Better still, if they sometimes during the day repeat this offering in a few words. For instance, when one is walking: "O my God, I wish that every step be an act of love for You."

What is to prevent us saying a few times every day: "O my God, every word I say I wish to be an act of love for You."

When writing we may pause for a moment and say to God: "My God, every word I write I wish to be an act of love for You."

Some ladies, when sewing, have the pious custom of saying, "O my Jesus, I wish that every stitch I give be an act of love for You."

The wonderful thing is that we thus make every act an act of great merit for ourselves. For every such act, we shall have a great reward in Heaven.

Our Lord said to one of His great servants: "Any Christian can make an act of love in a moment that will last for all Eternity."

Yet another time, He said: "One act of love gives Me more pleasure than a thousand hideous blasphemies give Me pain." Now if one mortal sin deserves the awful pains of Hell for all eternity, surely one act of love, one good act must obtain a great reward for all eternity in Heaven. For every little cup of water we give to a poor man in God's name, God gives an eternal reward.

No sin, however small, goes without punishment. For every idle word that man shall speak he shall have to render an account for it in the Day of Judgment. So no good act goes without its special reward.

What a wondrous thought! Every good act, no matter how small, will have an eternal reward in Heaven! This is what Our Lord tells us: "Taste and see how sweet My yoke is, how light My burden." God's Religion is truly most beautiful and consoling.

Surely, then, every intelligent Christian should make his Morning Offering with great attention and deliberation. It means only one short minute. It is, as we have explained, so easy.

If he does not do it, what countless merits he loses and what glory and love he takes from God.

To obtain the protection of God's Holy Mother we would do well to say daily this beautiful little prayer after the Morning Offering:

My Mother and my Queen, I offer to thee this day my eyes, my ears, my mouth, my heart, my head, my soul, my whole being. Since I belong to thee, dearest Mother, protect me as thine own property and possession.

Chapter 2

MORNING AND EVENING PRAYERS

Millions of Catholics are daily saying their morning and evening prayers. What a pity it is that so many of these millions do not give anything like the honor they could give to God, do not receive the immense benefits they could receive by these prayers.

Let us state a few facts which will enable our readers to say these prayers as they should.

The morning and evening prayers as given in the usual prayer books are chiefly five: The Our Father, the Hail Mary, the Apostles Creed, the Confiteor and the Hail Holy Queen, begun and ended with the Sign of the Cross. At night the Act of Contrition, for any faults of the day, is added.

These prayers only take five minutes when said reverently. Some are pleased to say longer prayers, but at least five minutes every morning and five minutes every evening is not too much to give to God.

Why are we here on earth? Why did God make us?

To know and love and serve Him for the few years we are on earth and so deserve to be with Him after this life forever in Heaven.

We have our duties, our work, our various occupations, but the first and greatest duty we have is to pray to God.

How can we say that we love and serve Him if we do not pray?

There are 24 hours in the day—five minutes given in the morning, five in the evening, is very little to give to God. Give Him this at least.

But these minutes must not be given by rushing over our prayers, pouring out words as if we were so many gramophones.

We must pray as intelligent beings.

Is it hard to pray well? By no means, as we have already explained. We know that God is infinitely good and loving, and that He is really our best friend. When we pray we are speaking to Him. He is looking at us and listening to us.

What do we say to Him? That is exactly what we are going to explain.

The five prayers are so beautiful and so simple that anyone can understand them if he only tries.

It is well to remember that one Sign of the Cross well made is of greater value than the same Sign made a thousand times hastily and irreverently.

One Our Father, one Hail Mary properly said, that is, as even the most simple person can say them, are of far greater value than a thousand Our Fathers or a thousand Hail Marys badly said.

We need not take much time, we need make no great effort to say these prayers.

All we are required to do is to know how to say them, know what they mean and know their immense value.

What, once more, we ask our dear readers to do is to read this book slowly and attentively and read it not once, but many times.

This is asking little if we, thereby, induce millions of Catholics to give greater glory to God, gain incomparably greater graces for themselves and obtain abundant blessings for their native country and for the whole world.

This seems all very wonderful, but if our readers will read carefully these few pages and try to put them into practice, what may seem difficult will prove to be very easy and of immense value.

Read the story of Sodom and Gomorrah and see what a few good men can do for a whole city.

God said to Abraham that if there were only ten good men found in these horrible dens of vice, He would spare the whole cities for their sakes.

But both cities were destroyed by fire from Heaven, simply because there were not ten men in them to pray to God.

The King of Nineveh saved his city—which God had threatened to destroy—by prayer.

Again, one virtuous woman, Judith, saved Bethulia and all its inhabitants from destruction.

It is incredible what one good man can do by his prayers. But if all our Catholics, or at least the greater number, would only say their daily prayers well they would most assuredly save the world from many and dire evils.

Let us then try to understand the wonderful

meaning of the prayers we say.

In the following pages we shall explain the meaning of these prayers. When saying them we cannot, of course, think actually of all the explanations, one by one, but if we have these clearly in our minds, if we fully understand them we shall pray with confidence, love and joy.

Three conditions give prayer its mighty power. First of all, **loving faith** and **confidence.** The Lord tells us that with a little faith we can move mountains.

Second, **perseverance,** for with perseverance we storm Heaven, as the Apostle tells us, and take it with violence.

Third, **humility,** which compels the Heart of Jesus to give us what we ask. Nothing pleases Him so much.

Chapter 3

THE SIGN
OF THE CROSS

We begin all our prayers with the Sign of the Cross. We must make this blessed Sign with reverence and respect, slowly—not too slowly—but certainly not with the irreverent haste with which many ignorant Christians make it.

It is the most holy and powerful sign man possesses. It drives the devil away, it helps us to banish temptations and protects us from the gravest dangers.

When well made it gives intense pleasure to God; made irreverently it is nothing else than a hideous caricature, an insult to Our Lord.

Well made it obtains for us great graces. Badly made it is mockery.

From the earliest times we find that the Sign of the Cross was used publicly as a protection against sickness, plagues and epidemics, against dangers of all kinds, in storms and in earthquakes.

All fervent Christians make the Sign of the Cross with the utmost confidence as a shield against every evil.

THE POWER OF
THE SIGN OF THE CROSS

In the reign of the Emperor Phocas, a Persian embassy arrived at the Imperial Court in Constantinople. These ambassadors and their suite were all Mohammedans. The Emperor and the members of the palace remarked that these Mohammedan princes and their followers had the Sign of the Cross marked on their foreheads.

Surprised at this love and respect for the Sign of the Cross on the part of fanatical Moslems, they inquired the reason.

The Moslems explained that some years previously a terrible epidemic had raged in Persia. The Moslems noted that the Christians signed themselves with the Sign of the Cross and were thus delivered from the plague.

Convinced of the power of the Cross, they themselves did likewise and were also delivered from the awful scourge.

Since then profound respect was shown for this holy Sign, which was considered as a protection and safeguard from sickness and pestilence.

Many devout Catholics, when troubled with any pain or sickness, make the Sign of the Cross with their thumb on the part afflicted saying, "By the holy Sign of the Cross deliver us, O Lord, from all evils and sickness."

This holy practice is of the greatest efficacy and should be used by all the faithful.

THE JEW AND THE SIGN OF THE CROSS

The following fact is authenticated by the highest authority.

A Jew was traveling on foot to Rome, and being suddenly overtaken at nightfall by a great storm took refuge in the ruins of a pagan temple. Wearied by his day's journey, he soon fell fast asleep.

At dead of night he was suddenly awakened by horrible noises and a suffocating odor. His horrified glance fell on a number of devils, whose hideous forms filled him with terror. Remembering that the Christians whom he knew used the holy Sign in all dangers, he too, as best he could, made the Sign of the Cross, which at once drove the devils in headlong flight from the temple.

On reaching Rome he recounted this fact, and the Holy Father ordered a rigorous examination of his statements to be made. These were shown to be perfectly true.

ST. HILARION CALMS THE SEA BY THE SIGN OF THE CROSS

After the death of the Emperor Julian, a fearful earthquake struck terror into the inhabitants of Peloponessus. This was followed by an upheaval of the sea which rose to an immense height and threatened every moment to destroy the city of Epidaurus. St. Hilarion approached the seashore and made the Sign of the Cross, when, at once, the sea sank back to its usual level and became calm and tranquil.

St. Benedict, when wicked men tried to kill him by giving him a cup of poisoned wine, made the Sign of the Cross over it and the goblet was at once shattered to pieces.

St. Louis Bertrand changed a gun pointed at him by a would-be assassin into a crucifix, by the Sign of the Cross.

Cyprian, a wealthy pagan who wished to marry a Christian lady named Justina, was incensed at her refusal to consider his proposals.

He employed the diabolical machinations of a well-known sorcerer, who assured him of success. However the efforts of this ally of the devil proved to be unavailing.

Cyprian upbraided him for his failure, whereupon the sorcerer confessed in self-defense that Justina was accustomed to make the Sign of the Cross, which frustrated all his diabolical efforts.

Cyprian, profoundly impressed by this confession, replied, "Your master, the devil, must indeed be weak and Christ very strong, therefore in future I will pay my allegiance to Christ, the Lord."

Faithful to his word he became a Christian and a great saint.

A CRIPPLE CURED BY THE SIGN OF THE CROSS

The holy Bishop, St. Bonnet, was once asked by a poor cripple to place his hand on his suffering members, hoping that the touch of the holy man would restore his limbs to their pristine health and strength.

"I will gladly do what you ask," replied the Bishop, "but it will avail you nothing."

He touched the poor, withered legs of the disabled man, but his touch produced no result, much to the disappointment of the infirm man.

Moved to compassion, St. Bonnet then said, "I will now do something which will give you back your strength." Stretching forth his hand, he made with it the Sign of the Cross and lo, in an instant the lame man was completely restored to health!

JULIAN THE APOSTATE

The impious emperor Julian the Apostate did not hesitate to hold communications with the devil.

On one occasion, accompanied by a noted magician, he entered a dark, subterranean cavern where the devil was wont to be honored.

Horrible noises greeted his affrighted ears. Hideous figures became visible in the gloom, so that the Emperor was terrified.

Mindful of the power of the Sign of the Cross, which he had so often made as a child, he now instinctively signed himself with this holy Sign.

Instantly the horrible noises ceased, the dreadful figures disappeared and all was peace.

The impious emperor, regaining his lost courage, once more attempted to perform the devilish rites, whereupon the devils again appeared and struck terror into his heart. Again, filled with fear, he made this holy Sign and the devils fled headlong from the cavern.

This episode is related both by St. Gregory and St. Augustine.

THE SAINTS AND THE SIGN OF THE CROSS

In the lives of the Saints we find other innumerable proofs of the power of the Sign of the Cross.

St. Dominic raised the dead to life by the holy Sign.

St. Vincent Ferrer worked hundreds of miracles by this blessed Sign.

Tertullian relates that the Christians in the first centuries began everything with the Sign of the Cross. When they left their homes or reentered them, they blessed themselves. Arising in the morning or going to rest at night, they made the Sign of the Cross with great devotion. In all dangers and temptations they made the same holy Sign.

St. Patrick made the Sign of the Cross 400 times a day.

All good Christians should strive to make the Sign of the Cross as frequently as possible.

By this blessed Sign, devoutly made, we give immense glory to God, for we offer to Him the infinite merits of the death of Jesus Christ.

But never, never should a Christian make the Sign of the Cross hastily or irreverently.

HOW SHOULD WE MAKE
THE SIGN OF THE CROSS?

The following explanations are of great importance:

Firstly, we should make the Sign of the Cross with the intention of renewing the Passion of Jesus Christ, of offering to the Eternal Father the infinite merits of the death of His Son—and this **in union with the Masses actually being said all over the world.**

The Mass is nothing else than the repetition, the renewal of Calvary. Therefore, when we make the Sign of the Cross we should distinctly wish to offer to God all the Masses being said all over the world.

When we make the Sign of the Cross in this manner we give unspeakably great glory to God and obtain, each time, immense graces for ourselves. We actually participate in the Masses being said all over the world!

Secondly, we should make the Sign of the Cross **to thank God,** with all our hearts, for having died for us.

How many men never once thank God for having suffered the awful death of Calvary for them! And yet, He died on Calvary for each one of us in particular. On the Cross, He clearly saw each one of us and offered all His pains, sufferings and Precious Blood for each of us!

Oh, then at least when making the Sign of the Cross let us wish with all our hearts to thank

God! Otherwise, we are guilty of the blackest
ingratitude.

Thirdly, we should make the Sign of the Cross
with the intention of applying to our souls the Passion of Jesus Christ.

Our Lord died for us, He offered the infinite
price of His Precious Blood for us; this is not sufficient unless we, ourselves, apply His merits and
Precious Blood to our own souls.

Alas, many Christians never think of doing this!

Fourthly, we should wish by this holy Sign to
drive the devil far from us, and to ask God by the
infinite merits of His Divine Son to deliver us from
all evils.

Fifthly, when we make the Sign of the Cross, we
say the words: "In the name of the Father and of
the Son and of the Holy Ghost."

What does this mean? By these words the Christian means to say:

1) I firmly believe in the Father, Son and Holy
Ghost.

2) I place all my unbounded trust and confidence in the Father, Son and Holy Ghost.

3) I love with all my heart the Father, Son and
Holy Ghost.

Said in this way, the words are a most fervent
act of faith, hope and love.

This holy Sign once made, as we have explained, is of more worth than the Sign of the Cross made hastily and irreverently a thousand times.

Therefore, Christian man who reads these lines, remember to make this holy Sign for the future with the full understanding of what you are doing.

Once more we call the attention of our readers to the fact that it **is not necessary to take a long time in making this holy Sign, but: a) we must understand and feel what we are doing, and b) we must make the holy Sign slowly and reverently.**

Chapter 4

THE OUR FATHER

The most beautiful prayer we have is that made and given us by God Himself. Each word, each thought was chosen especially by the infinite wisdom and love of God, and each is in itself a source of mercy and grace.

It is a key which God places in our hands to open His treasures, to open His Sacred Heart so that we may take what we want. If all the bishops and saints of the world were gathered together for a whole year and asked to compose a most efficacious and loving prayer, they could produce nothing as perfect as the Lord's Prayer. No wonder, therefore, that the Church commands it to be repeated so frequently.

Unfortunately, many of the faithful say it hurriedly and mechanically, not thinking of the meaning of the words, just repeating it as if they were so many talking machines. Is that fair to God? Is it fair to themselves? Is it intelligent? Is it reverent?

The Saints say that each part of the Our Father is an act of perfect love, and, as such, of the highest value and greatest merit. Let us examine the words in order that our readers may the more easily understand their beauty.

"Our Father." These two words are the most consoling words in the human language. The God of infinite love and goodness assures us by them that He is our Father in the truest, most affectionate and most intimate sense of the words. The love and affection of all the fathers and mothers who have ever lived, if compressed into one, would be a mere shadow compared to the tenderness, the love of God for each one of us. He loves each one as if that one were the only child He had on earth, as if he were the only one He had created, the only one He had redeemed. Think well, dear reader, on these words.

Giving us the prayer, He commands us to treat Him as the most confiding child treats its loving father. He does not merely ask in these words for adoration or veneration. What He wants is our real, affectionate and confiding love. He is offering us His love, and in return is asking us for ours.

Why not accept this loving invitation? God means what He says; it is He Himself who puts the expression in our mouths. We have only to take Him at His word.

We must, above all, when repeating these words, put away any thought of fear, for they are the expression, the revelation of God's most perfect love for us.

One of the great saints was, like St. Paul, transported in spirit into Heaven and saw the Eternal Father. She was, at first, afraid to look on His Divine Majesty, but when at His command she did so, all her fear gave place to the most intense love and delight. He was, indeed, divinely beautiful and glorious and full of majesty, but her soul was ravished incomparably more by the sight of His goodness, sweetness and love. Never could she forget that wondrous vision.

"Hallowed be Thy Name." By these words we praise and glorify and bless God for His great goodness to us. We wish and pray that He may be known and loved by all mankind, by Catholics and pagans, by Jews and Moslems. In these words there is nothing of self-interest. We are not thinking of, nor asking anything for ourselves. We are desiring and praying only that the good God may be known and loved as He deserves to be by all His creatures.

"Thy Kingdom come." This is surely a prayer that must appeal to us most strongly. What could be better for the world than that the Kingdom, which Christ came on earth to establish, should be founded everywhere and should flourish wherever it exists. By these words we pray that God's peace, God's love, God's law may reign supreme all over the world, especially in our own native land which is naturally so dear to us.

We must remember, too, in our prayers those countries where religion is so cruelly persecuted by the enemies of God. Prayer is the mightiest arm we can use against them. If all the millions of men who say the Our Father daily and many times in the day would each send up to the throne of God this burning petition, **"Thy Kingdom come,"** what help would they not win for those countries which are so cruelly tried!

By saying these words with devotion we are actively spreading the Gospel in all nations, carrying on the very work of the Apostles. By prayer, no less than by preaching, we can be apostles. In fact, preaching without prayer is of no avail.

Clearly St. Alphonsus is right when he says that these words are acts of most perfect love. What could be holier and better and more pleasing to God than this universal prayer poured forth by millions of hearts daily that His Kingdom be everywhere established and loved.

By them we may also have the intention of asking Him to take us to His own heavenly Kingdom after death, when the trials and sorrows of life are over. There we shall see Him face to face in the enjoyment of most perfect bliss. What better thing can we pray for, what holier thing can we desire than to be united with God forever in Heaven?

"Thy Will be done." The Will of God for us is perfect happiness. If we do His Will, we shall be perfectly holy and perfectly happy. If we wander ever so little from what He wills, we are sure to suffer. No one desires our welfare as He does. He, and He alone, can give happiness. It is, therefore, with the greatest fervor that we should pour forth these words: **"Thy Will be done."**

Not only should we say them with all our heart when repeating the Our Father, but we should use them frequently during the day in the form of an ejaculation, especially in sorrow or pain or disappointment.

They transform everything into gold for Heaven. If we wish to do all we do because God wills it— and it would be madness not to do so — our every work, our every individual act, our every pain and trouble and sorrow, becomes a merit, a treasure for Heaven, an act most pleasing to God. This seems about too good to be true, but it is the teaching of St. Thomas. It is true.

"Give us this day our daily bread." By these words we treat God with infinite confidence, a confidence resulting from the love we give Him, as our Father. We ask Him to give us all we need, all that is good for us, for body and soul, for ourselves and for those dear to us.

Is it not He who reminds us that He takes care of the little birds of the air, of the lilies of the field, but, that more, He will take care of us? Not even one hair falls from our heads without His permission.

When He was on earth did He not give sight to the blind, hearing to the deaf, cleanse lepers, console the sorrowful, do good to all? When we ask for our daily bread, we are asking for everything that we can possibly need.

"Forgive us our trespasses, as we forgive those who trespass against us." Here we ask God to forgive our sins, those awful sins that offend Him so much and do us such grievous harm on earth, and for which we shall have to suffer intensely in Purgatory.

How few know what calamities they bring on themselves by their sins! Lovingly, therefore, we ask God to pardon us everything, the great sins, the small sins, the pains too, and the punishment due to our sins. He has told us that even if our sins are as red as scarlet, He will make them as white as snow!

Let us weigh well the words: "as we forgive those who trespass against us." To obtain forgiveness for ourselves, we must forgive others.

We must ask Him to give us strength to sin no more, for it would be of little use to be forgiven if we went on sinning as before! If we ask Him humbly and confidingly, He will pardon us as He pardoned the poor publican in the Temple, the thief on the cross, Magdalen at His feet, all the poor sinners who have ever gone to Him. He came on earth expressly to pardon sin. "I came not for the just, but for sinners."

There is nothing that He loves more than to pardon sin and forgive His poor weak children. If we daily, in the Our Father, implore His pardon we shall deliver ourselves from much punishment in this life and in the next.

We do so little penance, we are afraid of it. It is repugnant to our natures. Let us at least say **fervently** each time we repeat the Our Father, "forgive us our trespasses." That will act at least in part as penance.

"Deliver us from evil." This last petition is deserving of our best attention. Many dangers threaten us, some known to us, others completely unforeseen. We meet with difficulties when we least expect them, such as sickness, loss of goods, the hostility of others. We are in a vale of tears. Suffering is what we have to expect. Against all these evils we ask our heavenly Father to deliver us, to protect us, to save us.

How many men and women have died in accidents, or have been swept off by epidemics, or died prematurely and are now lying in the cemeteries, who would still be happy in their homes had they lovingly asked God to protect them.

How many boys and girls are sinful and miserable, wasting away their days in jails and hospitals, who would be good and happy citizens if they had prayed to the Father above!

How many millions of souls are in Hell, who would now be high in Heaven, had they called on God with trust and love to deliver them from all evil.

Let us, then, throw special fervor into this last petition, "Deliver us from evil. Amen."

God never abandons those who trust in Him.

Chapter 5

THE HAIL MARY

How few of those who every day say the Hail Mary have an adequate idea of its beauty, a due comprehension of the wonderful graces it gives.

The Hail Mary comes down to us from the apostolic times. The Apostles used the *Pater Noster* and *Ave Maria* in the celebration of the Divine Mysteries.

Pope St. Clement, St. Basil, St. John Chrysostom, following this example, introduced the Hail Mary into the liturgies they established.

The words of the prayer are most beautiful and most simple. The humblest Catholic who says it on his beads can understand it, while it is so full of meaning that it offers food for contemplation to the brightest intellects.

St. Jerome says that the words of the Hail Mary are so sublime that no human intelligence is capable of adequately explaining them.

They contain the wondrous message of the Most Holy Trinity to Mary, which was delivered to her by the Prince of the Archangels and which conferred on her the dignity of Mother of God. This dignity is so high that, as St. Thomas says, she could not be raised to a higher one.

The Mystery embodied in the simple words of the Hail Mary is so far above all created comprehension that neither man nor angel could ever have dreamed of its possibility had not God revealed it.

St. Thomas Aquinas, the prince of theologians, spent a whole Lent preaching on the Hail Mary in Rome, and at the end of his conferences the great Doctor was far from having exhausted the subject.

The learned and holy Suarez declared, when dying, that he would willingly give all he had ever written for the merit of one Hail Mary.

Renan, without doubt an impartial judge, says that the story of the Annunciation, of which the Hail Mary is an abridgment, is one of the most beautiful pages in the world's literature.

OUR THOUGHTS WHEN SAYING THE HAIL MARY

When saying the Hail Mary we are repeating to Our Lady the very words of the Archangel St. Gabriel; we are giving her the message he brought her from the Holy Trinity, we are offering her anew all the joys and graces, the immense ocean of happiness that she received at the moment when she became Mother of God.

Our words give her the most intense joy. She hears them with a pleasure like to that which she heard them when they first fell from the lips of the angel.

Our Lord once said to St. Francis, "Francis, give Me something, give Me your love, your heart!"

The Saint replied, "I can give You nothing, Lord, for I have already given You all I have, all that I am."

Our Lord replied, "Give it to Me again Francis, and I will receive it with the same joy as when you gave it first."

So we, too, can offer to the sweet Mother of God, again and again, the joys, the graces she received when she was made Mother of God.

Mary is our Mother, a thousand times more our Mother than our earthly mother. It is the joy, the desire of a mother to give all she can to her children.

Let us offer her, each time we say the Hail Mary, all the wonderful joys and graces of the Annunciation, and let us ask her to give us in exchange a share, a great share, of the happiness and joys she then received.

Secondly, when we say the Hail Mary let us say with special attention the words: "Pray for us sinners, now and *at the hour of our death.*"

If we beg Our Lady all the thousands of times that we say the Hail Mary the grace of a happy death, she will surely be with us at that awful hour; she will surely drive the devil from our sides; she will surely, too, take us in her maternal arms and offer us to her Divine Son.

In the past we may have said these words without meaning, without emphasis. In the future let us say them with all our heart and with unlimited confidence in the love of Mary, for she is in truth our dearest Mother.

St. Gertrude tells us that when we pray to God and thank Him for the graces He has given to any saint, we are clothed, as it were, with the merits of that saint. And these merits are given us with so much love that they will be a cause of exceeding great joy to us for all eternity. And when we pray to any saint to obtain for us a happy death, God appoints that saint to be our special advocate to get us all we need.

What merits then may we not expect and what a most happy death will not be ours if we say frequently and devoutly the Hail Mary in honor of God's holy Mother.

The merit of even one Hail Mary is so great that, as we saw, the holy Suarez was ready to give all the great works he had written in exchange for the merit of one Hail Mary.

Chapter 6

THE POWER OF THE HAIL MARY

The following incidents recounted by St. Alphonsus Liguori and other saints will help us to understand better the great efficacy of the Hail Mary and to say it more devoutly.

A young girl was once imprudent and acted in such a way as gave the devil great power over her. He attacked her violently and even appeared to her in visible form. In terror she said the Hail Mary, whereupon he fled, never more returning to molest her.

Another unfortunate woman who had yielded to indecent liberties with a man who had vowed himself to God, found this unfortunate man hanging from the ceiling of his room. In despair, he had committed suicide.

Filled with remorse at the awful sight, she gave herself up to a life of penance and piety and finally entered a convent.

The devil, however, continued to tempt her cruelly. A holy Sister to whom she told her trouble advised her to say the Hail Mary with love and confidence. She did so and was delivered from all her fierce temptations.

The devil appeared to her and exclaimed in fury, "Accursed be she who told you how to say this prayer."

A pious legend tells how a very holy man was wont to say frequently the Hail Mary. In reward, Our Blessed Lady announced to him the day and hour of his death, when he died most holily.

After death a beautiful lily grew out of his mouth and on each of its petals was written the Hail Mary in letters of gold.

Cesarius relates that a humble brother knew no other prayer than the Hail Mary, which he loved to repeat.

After his death a tree grew over his grave and on its leaves were written the words: "Hail Mary, full of grace."

In Germany an unfortunate man, after a life of sin, was dying in despair. His confessor could not prevail on him to make his Confession.

Finally he induced him to say the Hail Mary. And at once the poor sinner recovered hope and made a good Confession.

DR. HUGO LAMMER AND THE *AVE MARIA*

On November 21, 1858, the learned Protestant theologian Dr. Hugo Lammer, of Brannsberg, embraced the Catholic Faith. Soon afterwards he became a priest, and in 1883 was made canon and professor of theology in Breslau. The cause of his conversion may be related briefly as follows:

He read an explanation of the Hail Mary and

was so pleased that he began to recite it daily.

Here are his own words: "I began to recite the sweet *Ave Maria,* and to implore Mary's powerful intercession for my speedy entrance into the True Church. The sting of intellectual conceit became extracted, and in my solitary dwelling, on my knees before the crucifix, I fought, with tears, many interior battles. Mary banished all scruples, and when later, I knocked at the door of the True Church, I could say with the greatest conviction *Credo* to every tenet of the Catholic religion."

The following true story is told by an English priest:

"One day a workman came to the presbytery, and asked to speak with me at once. He said that he was not a Catholic, but he would be very grateful if I would kindly visit his wife, who was very ill, and he believed that she had not very long to live. I asked him if she were a Catholic. 'No,' he answered, 'but she insists on seeing you, and will not hear of a clergyman of any other religion.'

"On reaching the house, I was welcomed most eagerly by the poor woman. She at once declared that she was convinced of the Catholic Truth, and begged me to instruct her in the doctrine of our religion. I was astonished at all this, for I learned that not one of her relations or neighbors were Catholics. I at once began my instruction.

"Before her death, she made her husband solemnly promise to become a Catholic, to send their children to the Catholic school, and to have them brought up in the Faith. After his wife's death, he faithfully carried out this promise. He declared that he owed his conversion mainly to the extraordinary patience and cheerfulness which his wife showed during her painful illness.

"Astonished at the exceptional graces the poor woman had obtained, I asked her if she had ever entered a Catholic church. Having received an answer in the negative, I continued: 'Have you ever spoken to a Catholic priest?' 'No.' she answered, 'When I was a little girl, I often played with Catholic children, and I learned a lovely prayer from them, which I have repeated every night, before going to bed.' Then she recited the Hail Mary; the secret was at last discovered. In the hour of death, Mary, her Heavenly Mother, had claimed her for her own in return for her love and fidelity in saying the Hail Mary."

Every time we say the Hail Mary we give to God's Blessed Mother immense pleasure. We in fact offer her anew all the joys and graces which she received when the Archangel Gabriel announced to her that she was made God's Mother.

When we say the Hail Mary we should say with great trust the words: "Pray for us, sinners, *now* (that is, during our life) and at the *hour of our death*." If we ask Our Lady every time we say the Holy Mary [the second part of the prayer] for a holy death, she will surely obtain it for us.

Chapter 7

THE CREED

It is quite true that Christians have a knowledge of what is contained in the Creed, but their knowledge is vague, abstract, it lacks conviction, does not give feeling, it is not effective. The proof of this is that so many Catholics have anything but a lively and active faith. And yet there is nothing so essential for our welfare as a realistic, solid, living faith.

The first grace we should ask for when saying the Creed is a lively faith. If we do so, we may be sure that, in return for all the Creeds we recite, God will grant us this ineffable gift.

Otherwise our faith will be reputed to us as a sin rather than a virtue, as a thing dead and useless and not a thing living and efficacious.

A good Catholic should have the idea of God and all concerning God vividly in his mind, in his heart, in his thoughts and in his life. Otherwise how can he consider himself a good Christian.

Let us dwell for a few moments on some of the words of the Creed.

"I believe in God, the Father Almighty." These are the first words of the Creed, and yet not one in a thousand who pronounces them says them with that feeling and comprehension he ought. They are said as a matter of routine.

The little story told of St. Thomas Aquinas as a boy will make our idea clear. He surely knew as well as any boy in his college who God was. Yet he asked his learned Benedictine professor, "What is God?"

He was not content with words, with vague thoughts—he wished to grasp the reality of God as far as mortal mind could grasp it. He was not content with mere abstract notions.

Yet the strength, consolation and joy of knowing so great and good a God is completely lost on many.

"And in Jesus Christ, Our Lord." The beautiful thoughts of the Incarnation that should fill our hearts to overflowing with gratitude are also unknown to many who say the Creed. Yet we repeat so frequently that the Son of God became man for us, that like any child of man He, the God Omnipotent, remained shut up in His Mother's chaste womb for nine whole months, that He lived on earth as one of us, for love of us, proving His love in countless ways.

This is like a legend to many. They do not *feel* it.

We repeat daily, and many times a day, that Christ suffered and died for each one of us, for me, for you who are saying the Creed, just as if you and I were the only ones for whom He died. What a thought!

Do we feel any gratitude, any love for Him in our heart of hearts? One thing is certain, we do not feel that overwhelming gratitude and love that we should feel if we had clear ideas, if we had solid convictions.

Do we ever sincerely thank Him for having died for us? No. We take it for granted. The truth has no repercussion in our souls. It is almost as if Christ had not died for us.

Then we say that we believe in the Holy Spirit, the Consoler, the Comforter, the Sanctifier. How little we know and love Him! Oh, if we only had the fervent wish when saying the Creed to ask Him for His gifts and consolations, how different our lives would be in every way!

We declare our belief in the Catholic Church. Have we any comprehension of the wondrous fact that we were born in, that we belong to the Catholic Church?

Millions and millions of men and women, Jews, Moslems, Buddhists, pagans, have never had the joy of knowing such a loving God, of practicing such a beneficent religion, of enjoying the hope of being with God forever and ever in Heaven. They never were assured that their sins were forgiven. They never once received God into their hearts as we may receive Him daily in Holy Communion.

What kind of faith have we? Do we sincerely thank God for placing us in the Catholic Church?

We believe also in the Communion of Saints. Not one in ten thousand understands this beautiful doctrine, the friendship and brotherhood of the angels and saints.

How few, for instance, treat their dear Guardian Angel with a semblance of the love and confidence with which they should. Yet he is always near us, always ready, longing to help us, defend and protect us.

We neither know him nor love him, nor enjoy his friendship, nor use his power to help us.

Our patron Saints, what do we know of them? Do we honor them and pray to them?

What good have we received from muttering the Creed so often, all these years back?

What a glorious, lively faith we should have if we only said the Creed well!

Of course, we cannot delay meditating on all the articles as we have been now examining them, in detail, but we should be impregnated at least with the ideas. We should have a deep feeling of what we are saying.

Sometimes, too, we should say the Creed slowly, in the spirit we have explained. It would serve as a beautiful and most practical meditation. This was how St. Teresa loved to say it.

In truth, what act of faith can equal that framed for us by the Apostles and said daily for so many centuries by the millions of the faithful.

It is well, therefore, to have the wish when saying the Creed:

1) To offer to God all the faith of the Apostles, the faith of the countless missionaries who have at all times labored, and are still laboring, to spread the Faith in pagan lands.

2) To offer to God all the blood of the countless martyrs who have suffered in testimony of their faith, and who are even now, in various parts of the world, bearing witness to God with heroic fortitude and generosity.

3) To offer to God the faith of all the Catholics who are daily reciting the Creed all over the world.

4) To ask for a lively, strong, comprehensive faith for ourselves.

The Creed said in this way will soon produce abundant fruits in our souls.

These suggestions are clearly only a few of the many that might be made. The reader can use one or all of them at his good pleasure.

If they are adopted, the Creed will be said with incalculably greater benefit than by rushing over it mechanically, as we have perhaps been doing for many years.

Chapter 8

THE CONFITEOR

Few Christians know how to say the Confiteor.

There is no sin God hates as much as pride, and no virtue He loves more than humility. It was pride that hurled millions of glorious angels into Hell. It was pride, too, that drove our first parents from Paradise.

At all times pride has been the ruin and curse of man. God loves to humble the proud.

Even we ourselves feel a dislike for the proud and arrogant. They are repugnant to us, their pride and vanity repel us.

On the other hand, humility charms us. We love and feel at home with those who are modest and unassuming. Much more does God love the humble and detest the proud.

Jesus Christ, the Son of God, teaches us humility by His every act.

He was born in a stable, He was poor, He loved the poor, He lived with the poor. He chose to be unknown for 30 years, hidden away from the gaze of men, known as the carpenter's son. What insults and ignominy did He not choose to suffer in His Passion!

One of His principal commands, to the practice of which He attaches a great reward, is: "Learn of Me because I am meek and humble of heart and you will find peace to your souls."

Learn of **God** to be humble!

His blessed Mother was most dear to Him because of her humility. At the greatest, the most glorious moment of her existence, when she was made Mother of God, she abased herself by an act of profound humility: "Behold the handmaid of the Lord."

Never in all her life did a shadow of pride pass over her soul.

All the Saints, from the greatest to the least, were saints in proportion as they were humble.

What a revelation to us is the story of the Pharisee and the Publican! It dispenses with comment. The Pharisee, notwithstanding all his good works, was condemned because of his pride. The Publican, though a sinner, was pardoned and sanctified because of that most precious act of humility: "Lord, have mercy on me, a sinner."

Wondrous words, which even now win plenary pardon for the sinner who repeats them with confidence and humility.

The thief on the cross, as a reward of one humble act of contrition was—notwithstanding a lifetime of crime—admitted that very day to Heaven: "This day thou wilt be with Me in Paradise."

The touching story of the Chananean woman is

another example of how much Our Lord loves humility.

This poor woman begged Jesus to cure her child. Our Lord did not even answer her!

She persisted. Jesus said: "I was only sent to the lost sheep of Israel."

She replied. "O Lord, do help me!"

"It is not good," Jesus said, "to throw the bread of the children to the dogs."

And she replied: "Yea Lord, but the dogs eat of the crumbs that fall from the master's table."

Then, indeed, did Our Lord look on her with wondrous love, exclaiming, "Oh, woman, great is thy faith! Be it done to thee according as thou wisheth."

In the Old Testament we have striking examples of how God is pleased by humility.

Because Achab, one of the most wicked kings of Israel, humbled himself, the awful penalties pronounced on him by God as a consequence of his sins were withheld.

Heli in consequence of an act of humility was, as so many of the Holy Fathers think, saved, though his sins had called out to God for vengeance.

God sent his prophet Jonas to Nineveh to tell its people that the city would be destroyed in three days, because of its awful sins. The King, hearing the divine threat, humbled himself and commanded all his people to do likewise.

As a result they were pardoned and the city was spared.

HOW TO SAY THE CONFITEOR

When we say the Confiteor we should humble ourselves profoundly and sincerely before God, His Blessed Mother and the Saints.

This act, if sincere, is of the highest possible value. We should say the words with conviction, attend to their meaning and feel that we are in truth confessing our sins to God.

Let us have the intention of offering to God the humility of Jesus Christ, the humility of His Blessed Mother, the humility of all the Saints, to make up for our own want of humility. Many find it hard to be humble, yet it is *the secret* of happiness.

We forget or neglect to make acts of humility. Let us at least use the Confiteor as an act of sincere, profound humility, and this each time we say it.

Only in Heaven shall we realize the value of this great virtue.

Chapter 9

HAIL HOLY QUEEN

The Hail Holy Queen is the most beautiful hymn of praise and love that any child of Holy Mary has ever composed in her honor.

It is an outpouring of the human heart, an expression of the deepest feeling, combining sweetness, confidence, hope and love.

It is not certain who the author was, but whoever he was, we bless and thank him for this beautiful anthem.

It is ascribed by some to Hermann Contractus, by others to Peter, Bishop of Compostella, and by a third group of critics to Adhemar, Bishop of Puy. It began to be known in the eleventh century.

St. Bernard dearly loved it. Some say that it was he who added the last words: "O clement! O loving! O sweet Virgin Mary!"

The Dominicans were the first to recite the Hail Holy Queen after Compline by the order of St. Dominic himself.

The devil, seeing the wonderful good everywhere done by these white-robed friars, sought with satanic malice to disturb their devotions and the peace of their convent homes.

St. Dominic's successor, Blessed Jordan of Saxony, resolved to have recourse to her who had so frequently befriended the Order.

Instead of reciting the *Salve,* he ordered that a procession should be formed after Compline each evening, at which the *Salve* should be sung.

This devotion produced the most wonderful results. All the diabolical disturbances ceased, and abundant blessings were showered on the Order.

Later on the *Salve* was recited after all the Hours of the Office, and it was also ordained that on the occasion of the death of any member of the Order the community was to be assembled and the Hail Holy Queen sung around the bed of the dying brother.

Our Blessed Lady appeared more than once during the singing of the anthem and manifested her pleasure to the brethren. No wonder, then, that in their worldwide missions the Dominican preachers propagated most earnestly devotion to the Hail Holy Queen.

Godet in the "Revue du Clergé Français," of August 1910, basing his statement on several weighty authorities, affirms that the wonderful popularity of the Hail Holy Queen is due in the main to the zeal of the Friars Preachers.

St. Alphonsus has written an exhaustive explanation of the Hail Holy Queen in his beautiful little book: *The Glories of Mary.*

We shall confine ourselves to a few devout comments as a help to the devotion of our readers.

"HAIL HOLY QUEEN"

Our Blessed Mother is not styled gracious, glorious or powerful Queen, though she has the right to all these titles. We say rather "Hail **Holy** Queen." She is the Immaculate Queen of Heaven, high above the Patriarchs and Prophets, above the cherubs and seraphs who stand before the throne of God.

"She is raised so far above all others," says St. Albert the Great, "that she is on a level, a plane of her own, below God but far above all creatures," higher, holier, greater than all others put together.

"MOTHER OF MERCY"

Mary's great prerogative is mercy. St. Alphonsus tells us that Jesus Christ has divided His Kingdom with His Blessed Mother. He made her Queen of Mercy.

Jesus came to us through Mary, so He wishes that all His mercies, graces, and favors come also through her.

St. Bernard says that it was never heard of in any time, in any place that Mary refused a grace to anyone who called on her for help, were he even the worst of sinners.

How often has it happened that a poor sinner, whose life has been one long crime, lies dying without God, without Sacraments, without friends, abandoned, alone.

The demons stand around his bed, watching his

labored breathing, waiting for his last breath, when he shall be theirs forever. Weaker and weaker he grows. One moment more and he is irretrievably lost.

But a long-ago memory, a thought of Mary flashes through his mind. He sends up one cry, one faint but confiding cry to his Mother in Heaven. She hastens to his side. He is saved.

"HAIL TO OUR LIFE, OUR SWEETNESS AND OUR HOPE"

What more tender, affectionate, confiding language could we use?

We tell our Blessed Mother that she is everything to us, and in truth she is. Tender was her love, vigilant her care for the Divine Child. Likewise tender and vigilant is she in regard to us. We are truly her children, given to her by Jesus, saved at the cost of His Precious Blood.

"TO THEE DO WE CRY POOR BANISHED CHILDREN OF EVE. TO THEE DO WE SEND UP OUR SIGHS, MOURNING AND WEEPING IN THIS VALLEY OF TEARS!"

The weakness of our first mother, Eve, condemned us to banishment in this vale of tears, in this world of sickness, sorrow and care where all is labor and struggle, trial and temptation.

God, in His surpassing goodness, has given us His own sweet Mother to console us, to help us, to wipe away our tears.

What madness not to place all our trust in Mary?

"SHOW UNTO US THE FRUIT OF THY WOMB, JESUS"

At the dread hour of death, when dark clouds gather round us and terror fills our souls; when the demons redouble their efforts in a last desperate effort to destroy us and the struggle against Hell is at its fiercest, oh then, dearest Mother, hasten to our help, be with us in our hour of need and show unto us the fruit of thy womb, Jesus.

"O CLEMENT, O LOVING, O SWEET VIRGIN MARY"

Help me in life, in my every need, in my every sorrow, but help me above all, dearest Mother, at the hour of my death.

Let us offer the Hail Holy Queen *every time we say it* to ask Mary to obtain for us a holy death. If we do so we shall, indeed, have happy deaths.

Chapter 10

THE GLORIA PATRI

One of the most beautiful prayers of the Church consists in the frequent repetition of the *Gloria Patri* which, though not divinely inspired as are the verses of the *Psalms,* is nevertheless considered by the great Saints and Doctors to be a most perfect and sublime form of praising God.

By it we wish to offer the Father, Son, and Holy Ghost the same praise and glory that the Holy Trinity offers to Itself—from the beginning, now, and forever. No creature can offer to God a prayer more holy and pleasing than this one.

It goes back to the Apostolic times and was introduced into the Office at a very early date.

When repeating it, we are uniting our voices with those of the heavenly hosts, who are ever singing the eternal *Sanctus, Sanctus, Sanctus, Domini Deus Sabaoth.*

St. Dominic, St. Francis of Assisi, St. Charles Borromeo and many other saints felt extraordinary joy and exultation in repeating the *Gloria*, so that their faces became radiant with a joy they could not hide or conceal from the eyes of others. St. Francis de Sales wrote an admirable explanation of the value of the *Gloria Patri* in his *Treatise*

On the Love of God, which is well worth perusing.

We, too, can enjoy immense consolation when repeating these wondrous words. They present no difficulty, and demand no mental effort.

1) All that is required is to understand the words and remember, when repeating them, that we are offering to the most Holy Trinity a most perfect act of love. We are offering in it not merely all the praises of the Angels and Saints, but the praise the Holy Trinity offers to Itself.

2) Some, when saying the *Gloria Patri,* imagine themselves standing in the midst of the blessed Angels and Saints, looking on the unveiled beauty of the Godhead. This beautiful thought gradually gives them an idea of Heaven, a foretaste of its joys, a feeling of intimacy with God never felt before.

3) Others, like St. Magdalen de Pazzi, offer their necks to the sword of the executioner, as the martyrs of old. No act of praise can be more pleasing to God than the offering of our blood and our life for His sake. Every time they say the *Gloria* they offer most solemnly and deliberately their blood and their lives to God.

Who knows but that God in His goodness will give them the glorious palm of martyrdom in some way or other. There are hidden martyrs, as there are hidden saints of all kinds. One may become a martyr in many different ways.

Bl. Bartholomeo of the Martyrs, the celebrated Archbishop of Braga, one of the most illustrious of the Fathers of the Council of Trent, felt a flood of joy fill his soul and his face lighted up when he recited the *Gloria Patri*. His was indeed an act of most perfect love.

5) Bl. Jordan of Saxony repeated the *Gloria Patri* with the ardor of a seraph, and frequently besought at this moment the all-powerful protection of the Blessed Trinity. Wondrous were the graces he received as a result.

6) Many devout Christians have the intention of making a most profound act of faith, confidence and love in the Holy Trinity when repeating these words.

They wish to profess their firm, living faith in the Father, Son, and Holy Ghost, as though they gazed on the Divine Persons in Heaven.

They place their fullest confidence and trust in the all-powerful help of the Three Persons, which they beg for most earnestly, as did Bl. Jordan.

They wish to love and bless and thank the Eternal Father for having created them to His own image and likeness; the Son for having redeemed them with His sufferings and death; and the Holy Ghost for consoling and sanctifying them.

Alas, how many might forget or neglect to make these great, essential acts were it not for their devotion in saying the *Gloria Patri*.

7) Others again wish to make reparation for the insults offered to God that day. How beautiful!

The devout recital of the *Gloria Patri* has another great value. It brings back our wandering attention, enkindles our love and gives a new impulse to our devotion.

We cannot, of course, dwell on all these various thoughts each time we say the *Gloria Patri*, but if our minds are full of the divine significance and grandeur of the words, our devotion will be secured.

It is a good method to select one or other thought for a month at a time. We may even dwell always on the same thought. This plan eliminates all difficulty.

It is a commendable practice too, to bow our heads devoutly when reciting the *Gloria Patri*. It increases our love and devotion.

It would, indeed, be difficult to overrate the importance of reciting these wonderful words of the Doxology with due reverence and comprehension.

Chapter 11

THE ROSARY

After morning and evening prayers, the next great duty of the good Christian is to say his daily Rosary.

No words can sufficiently explain the importance of this duty. It obtains countless blessings for those who perform it faithfully; it delivers them from innumerable dangers and evils of all kinds. During life it guarantees them a large measure of happiness and will most certainly insure them a most holy and happy death.

The reason why some lax and indifferent Catholics neglect the Rosary is simply because they have no idea of its value, what it is and how to say it.

We will explain some of the leading features of this wonderful prayer in the hope of convincing our readers not only to say the Rosary daily, but to say it with pleasure and devotion. They must, however, weigh well the facts that we adduce. If these are read with care, they will convince any sane and enlightened Catholic that he must say his Rosary. If perused in a hasty and superficial way, they will produce no good effect whatever.

THE ROSARY,
THE GREAT PRAYER OF THE CHURCH

Wherever a church is built, wherever Mass is said, wherever a missionary preaches the Gospel, there the Rosary is said.

Millions and millions of men and women all over the world say the Rosary. In every great city, town and village, in every Catholic home, in the cabin of the peasant, in the palaces of the rich, in the chapel of the Pope himself the Rosary is said.

Every day, every hour, in all the languages of the world, English, Irish, Americans, Spaniards, Portuguese, Italians, Germans, Poles, Chinese, Japanese, and the wild tribes of Africa and Asia are sending up their *Ave Marias,* in a worldwide chorus, to their Heavenly Mother.

For the past 700 years since St. Dominic received the Rosary from the hands of Mary, Popes, Bishops, Saints, apostles, missionaries, priests in the pulpit and confessors in the confessionals have been and are constantly urging the people to say the Rosary.

And remark that not only the great masses of the faithful, but men most eminent in science, art and letters, lawyers, doctors and professors are saying their Rosary every day.

Why? Simply because they feel and know that it is the infallible source of all blessings and a sure safeguard against sin and evil.

Dear reader, we ask you frankly and clearly, will you dare to take up a stand against these millions and millions of magnificent, intelligent, and virile Christians? Are you so careless of your welfare on earth, of your eternal salvation, hereafter, have you so little love and respect for God's Blessed Mother that you will refuse to say the prayer that she herself gave you and begs you to say? Will you turn your back on her and despise her help?

Or, do you prefer to ally yourself with those unhappy, lax, indifferent Catholics who do not say the Rosary?

The Rosary is so easy, it can be said in five to six minutes! Dare you say that you cannot and will not give these minutes in exchange for inestimable blessings and happiness? Far from losing time, the Rosary will enable you to do very much more and better work, there will be peace in your home and your business will prosper.

ARE WE BOUND TO SAY THE ROSARY?

No, we are not bound by any special law or commandment but, as we have just said, and it is well to engrave it clearly on our hearts, the Popes, the Bishops of the whole world, the Saints, apostles, priests and missionaries, God's own Mother herself beg us to say it.

The Christian man or woman who knowingly and deliberately refuses to accept such counsel and advice is foolhardy in the extreme.

No sane man is so foolish as to discard a fortune offered to him, no man with the use of his senses will throw his money into the sea.

Now the Rosary is the greatest gift, the greatest

blessing, the greatest treasure that God's Mother could give us.

She promises her most special love, friendship and protection to all who say the Rosary!

She is so powerful with God that He never refuses her what she asks. She loves us so much that she can refuse us nothing we ask her through the Rosary.

There was never a sinner so hardened in crime, there was never a heart so broken with sorrow, never anyone so weak that Mary did not help and save and comfort if they only asked her.

IS THE ROSARY A TEDIOUS PRAYER?

1) Far from it, it is such a lovely, consoling, infallible prayer that even enlightened Protestants confess that the author of the Rosary must have been a profound student of human nature, for this prayer answers so admirably all human needs.

Only those who have never learned to say the Rosary properly can think the Rosary tedious.

2) Every Rosary we say with simple faith and devotion obtains for us such immense graces that only in Heaven shall we understand them.

What abundance of grace, then, will not the Rosaries we have been saying all our lifetime obtain for us?

3) The Rosary **well said** is quite enough to make a man a saint and to obtain plenary pardon for all his sins. How many Christians are ignorant of this wonderful truth? It is only necessary

to think on what we have already said of the Our Father and the Hail Mary to form an idea of what these graces are. Say your Rosary and say it well.

4) Which of us should not wish to have stood by the side of St. Bernadette in Lourdes or near Sr. Lucia in Fatima when they saw and conversed with Our Lady?

But when saying the Rosary, we are truly and really speaking to Mary. She is truly and really listening to us and ready to grant us all her favors. This is the way, the only true way of saying the Rosary, to know and feel that we are speaking to God's own Mother. If we say it in this way there will be no monotony, no weariness.

We will presently explain the new and wondrous graces that are to be obtained by the meditation, or thinking on the Mysteries, which is the very essence of the Rosary and which gives it a new charm, a new power.

WHO GAVE US THE ROSARY?

It was God's Mother who gave us the Rosary.

When we are shown the masterpiece of any great painter such as Raphael, Michelangelo, Titian or Angelico, we know at once that it is a work of priceless value and perfection.

Yet who are all the greatest masters in the world in comparison with God's Mother?

She is holier, more wise, more powerful than all the Angels and Saints. She is the greatest, the mightiest, the wisest of all God's creatures.

Let us bear clearly in mind that the Rosary is not only the gift of God's Mother, but that it is her masterpiece.

She gave us two great gifts. First of all, she gave us her Divine Son, Jesus. Secondly, she gave us the Rosary.

The Son of God made man came to us through Mary. We have to go to God through Mary; she it is who takes us and gives us to God.

She does this by the Rosary, which is a prayer so powerful, so infallible, planned as it was, with all her wisdom and power and love!

She gave us the Rosary to make us good, to make us strong, to make us happy, to make us holy.

God gives us all His graces through Mary, and she gives us these graces most especially through the Rosary.

It is simply a most perfect work, so perfect that Mary could not give us anything better.

She gave it to us as a sure and certain means of obtaining *everything* we need, as a means to conquer the devil, as a means to overcome all our weaknesses and temptations.

WHAT WAS MARY'S PLAN IN GIVING US THE ROSARY?

Our Lord came down on earth to teach us a most beautiful and holy religion, a religion specially made to help and comfort our poor human hearts, a religion at the same time so divine that it transforms poor weak men into angels of perfection, if they only practice it.

Jesus when on earth gave us the most beautiful lessons, the most sublime and beneficent doctrines, the wisest counsels and commandments, everything that could possibly make us holy and happy.

But from the beginning, men placed obstacles to His holy religion and thus for many, very many, it became useless. It was for them as if God had never come.

First of all they forgot quickly what He had taught.

Then they did not understand His beautiful teaching, His love and His goodness.

Thirdly, they were weak and they easily fell away and, as a consequence, innumerable souls were lost.

The Blessed Mother of God planned the Rosary to remedy these three evils.

In the Rosary, all the beautiful doctrine, teaching and lessons of Jesus Christ are divided into fifteen great points which we call Mysteries.

These fifteen points are as it were a resumé of Christ's teaching. In them we think on His life, death and Resurrection.

Each Mystery contains a number of practical lessons, reminds us of our everyday duties, keeps before our minds the Christian virtues, and this in a way admirably suited to all classes, the most humble and the most cultured. All is simple, all is clear, each one drinks of the fountains of living waters according to his needs.

By saying the Rosary, therefore, every day we

cannot possibly forget the teaching of Our Lord, for it is always before our eyes. We cannot forget the great Mystery of the Incarnation, the sufferings and death of Our Lord, His glorious Resurrection.

Better still, as our minds are slow in grasping truths, the more we think of these Mysteries, the more clearly, the more profoundly we understand the beauty and grandeur of God's holy religion.

Thirdly, because the truths Our Lord teaches us are supernatural and divine, we need divine light and grace to grasp them and strength to practice them.

When we are thinking on the fifteen Mysteries we are praying, we are saying the Our Father and Hail Mary. These powerful, irresistible prayers obtain for us the light and faith to feel and understand the Mysteries, the teaching of Our Lord. They also obtain for us strength and courage and perseverance to practice all Christ's holy lessons.

What a beautiful, divine, comprehensive plan has not Our Lady given us in the Rosary, truly worthy of her wisdom and love.

The greatest saints loved to think on, to ponder on these Mysteries, and the more they thought on them the more they grasped their divine meaning, and as they thought and pondered their hearts burned with love, and a new and strange strength and energy gave them power to reach the highest sanctity.

We shall see in the following incidents that not

only the Saints, but the most humble of the faithful derive the like benefits from the meditations of the Mysteries.

Chapter 12

THE OLD IRISH WOMAN'S ROSARY

Lady Beatrice Allen, a noble and wealthy English lady, an ardent Protestant by conviction, once accosted a poor Irish woman whom she found saying her Rosary.

In the hope of converting "the poor benighted creature," as she considered her, good Lady Beatrice asked the poor woman why it was that she said that silly prayer.

"Silly prayer, my Lady, you call it, but it is for me my joy and consolation.

"When I am sad and sorrowful it consoles me, and when I am well and happy it gives me more joy and pleasure.

"How could it be silly, my Lady, to speak to the Holy Mother of God, and sure that is what I am doing when I say the Rosary."

"Well then," replied Lady Beatrice, "will you tell me all about it?"—quite sure that she was going to hear a story of gross superstition.

The explanation of the Rosary which this poor vendor of vegetables gave Lady Beatrice was so clear and, withal, so impressive that she afterward confessed that she had never heard from bishop or dean of her religion a sermon that gave her more to think about.

Weeks passed and months passed and she could not get the words of the old woman out of her mind, much as she tried. It was all so simple, so true, so sincere.

Sufficient to say that our noble lady put herself under instruction and was received into the Catholic Church at the end of a year.

This caused terrible trouble in her up-to-then happy home. Her husband and friends thought she was mad. During the bitter struggle that ensued, Lady Beatrice never abandoned the Rosary that she had so well learned to say and love and, at the end of the second year, her husband and children joined the Church!

Here is briefly how the dear, old, unlettered woman preached her sermon on the Rosary.

Holding up her beads to Lady Beatrice, she showed her the crucifix and said: "When I begin to say my beads, my Lady, I kiss the five Wounds of Jesus Christ as His holy Mother did when He was taken down from the Cross and placed in her arms. I thank Him for all He suffered for me, and I beg Him to pardon my sins and take me to Heaven after my death.

"Then, as you see, my Lady, there are two parts in the Rosary: one is small and has only five beads.

"That tells me that life is short and that my sufferings will be soon over, and that I had better be ready for I may die any day, and I pray for a happy death.

"There is the big part, the five decades, and that reminds me of the long life that is to come that will never end. And I say to myself, 'Take care, Bridget Murphy, that you go to Heaven and not to Hell.' And I try my best to be good and not to offend God.

"On the big beads we say the Our Father, the prayer that God Himself gave to us. He must hear us, for sure He promised to do so. It was He who put the words into our mouths, and He must be our Father if He says it.

"Oh, it's a beautiful prayer and I love to say it! To think that God is my Father! That is enough to make anyone happy.

"On the small beads we say the Hail Mary, and that prayer, too, came from God for it is what the Angel Gabriel said to the Blessed Virgin when he told her that she was to be the Mother of God.

"Oh, how pleased the Blessed Virgin must be to hear again the self-same words of the angel, for I wish with all my heart to give her again the happiness and joy the angel gave her! She is my Mother, and I make bold to ask her to give me some of her great joy and holiness, for a true mother gives everything to her children.

"In the Hail Mary, I ask the Blessed Mother to pray for me, her poor child, now, during this hard and wearisome life, to help me in all my little troubles, but above all I ask her to pray for me when I am dying, at **the hour of my death.** Amen.

"Now, my Lady, how could God's Mother, who is

so good and sweet, refuse to listen to my poor prayers?

"I know she hears me, I am sure of it, and I am never tired saying the Hail Marys and giving her pleasure."

"But you must be tired repeating all those Hail Marys," queried Lady Beatrice.

"I am never tired, my Lady, of speaking to the Mother of God.

"I now want to explain to you that when we are saying the holy prayers we are thinking of how Our Lord became man and lived for 33 years on earth. These we call the Joyful Mysteries.

"After that we think of all His terrible sufferings and how He died on the Cross. These are the Sorrowful Mysteries."

Here the good woman became wonderfully eloquent, talking about the Passion and death of Jesus Christ. She felt all she said, for her poor voice became broken and tears ran down her cheeks.

"Last of all, my Lady, we think of how Our Lord rose up from the dead, glory be to God, and how He went to Heaven. These are the Glorious Mysteries.

"But before going, He told St. Peter and the other Apostles that He would send down the Holy Ghost to comfort and console them and us all and that He Himself would be always with us to help us.

"And truth He is in the Blessed Sacrament which we have in the Church. Every morning I go to Mass and poor and bad as I am, the priest tells me that I must go to Holy Communion.

"And I say the Joyful Mysteries and I think that the good God comes into my heart as He did when He went into the womb of the Blessed Virgin herself, and I ask her to help me to receive my God as she herself did. And I am sure she does, for I feel such comfort and peace."

Lady Beatrice listened in wonder and asked the old woman: "Who taught you all these wonderful things?"

"It was the nuns at home in Ireland where I went to school and the parish priest, Fr. O'Toole, God be merciful to him. He had a great way with him and used to explain everything very clearly."

It was Lady Beatrice herself who told us this story, but at much greater length and with many more details which, due to our limited space, we cannot give in all their fullness.

She loves to tell to priests the story of her conversion, and she wears on her arm the old Irish woman's rosary in the form of a bracelet. She treasures this as one of her most prized possessions.

From this fact we see how the Rosary can give to the humblest of the faithful a clear grasp and understanding of the great Mysteries of our Faith.

THE HOLY MARY AND A HAPPY DEATH

The following incident shows the power of the Hail Mary in obtaining for us a happy death.

Msgr. Dupanloup relates that, when still a simple priest, he was called to the deathbed of the young Duchess of Laus. He found the friends of the Duchess plunged in the profoundest grief.

Fr. Dupanloup was conducted to the presence of the dying lady. She was only 22 years of age, ideally happy and loved by all around her. She naturally clung to a life that promised so well for her.

The good priest was very tactful. He asked her if she would care to receive Our Lord, who could so easily, if He wished, restore her to health.

"Father," she said, "do please tell me if I am dying, do not fear to tell me the whole truth, I am quite ready to die."

"You are very, very ill," he replied.

"Thank God," she said. "I am not afraid. I am only sorry for my dear husband, who adores me."

"But how, my child," said the priest, "are you so prepared to die?"

"Well, Father," she said, "since my First Communion I have said my Rosary every day and in every Hail Mary I offered God's dear Mother the wondrous joys of her Annunciation. In every Hail Mary I said devoutly: 'Pray for us sinners now and at the hour of our death.' Fifty times every day for all these years I have asked God's dear Mother for a happy death.

"I am sure, perfectly sure that I am going to have a most happy death, and that God's sweet Mother is only waiting to take me in her arms to Heaven." Hers was, indeed, a most beautiful death.

THE ROSARY IN CHINA

China has been the scene of many cruel persecutions against the Church. On one of these occasions the bishops and priests in one of the missions were massacred to a man. Not one was left to minister to the faithful.

Only after 150 years were other missionaries able to arrive in this remote district. Great was their surprise to find a band of zealous Christians who still retained the Faith and had a reasonable grasp of the truths of our holy religion.

After diligent inquiries, they ascertained that these faithful sons of the Church had kept alive their faith by the recitation of the Rosary and meditating on its Mysteries.

Not many years ago, a venerable Franciscan bishop returned after long years spent in China.

He told us that the Chinese where he ministered had an extraordinary love and devotion to the Rosary.

When a father wished to praise his son he invariably said, "Oh, Father, this boy always says his Rosary." That was the best guarantee of his being a good boy.

The gift the people most loved to receive was rosary beads. Their eyes sparkled with joy, their faces were radiant with happiness, it was a real pleasure to see them so genuinely satisfied.

In Confession the missionaries soon learned that the penance most liked was the Rosary.

In fact, his lordship remarked, they seemed still

more pleased if the priest told them to say two or three Rosaries.

Chapter 13

THE POPES AND THE ROSARY

When the Holy Father is pleased to give his personal approval to a book, or write a letter in praise of any work, such a mark of honor is looked on as the highest honor that an author can receive, the best guarantee that any work can have.

It is not, however, one pope who has approved of and recommended the Rosary. Innumerable pontiffs have, since the time of St. Dominic, published decrees, rescripts, letters, approvals of every kind, couched in the most eloquent and impressive language, in favor of the Rosary. We quote some of these encomiums.

"By means of the Rosary immense benefits are every day being received by Christian peoples." (Urban IV).

"The Rosary was especially given us as a protection against the great evils and dangers that threaten the world." (Leo X).

"With the Rosary we drive the devil far from us." (Adrian VI).

"By the Rosary, St. Dominic appeased the anger of God against France and Italy." (Paul II).

Boniface VIII placed such unbounded confidence in the Rosary that he wished to be buried in vestments on which were embroidered the Mysteries of the Rosary. This act of filial confidence was so pleasing to God that his body was found incorrupt after 300 years.

Clement VIII was the author of no less than 19 bulls in favor of the Rosary. When he was elected Pope and proceeded to change his cardinal's robes for the papal dress, it was remarkable that he searched diligently in his pockets to find his rosary.

Now if one letter, or rescript, or encyclical of a pope carries with it so much weight and authority, why is it that pope after pope, including the latest popes, are constantly publishing other new and numerous bulls and briefs on the Rosary?

The reason is that the Rosary is so important, so necessary, so wonderful a prayer that the Popes can never do enough to make it known and loved.

It is well worthy of note that far from lessening their zeal, some of the recent Popes have even exceeded their predecessors in their proofs of confidence and love for the Rosary.

Pius VI, though weighed down under a very heavy load of care and sorrow, said the fifteen Mysteries of the Rosary every day.

Gregory XVI not only said the Rosary most fervently, but marched in the Rosary processions in the streets of Rome.

Pius IX, the great Pope of the Infallibility and of the Dogma of the Immaculate Conception, one of the holiest and greatest pontiffs who has governed the Church, says:

"The Rosary is a very treasure of graces. If you desire to have peace in your hearts, peace in your home, peace in your native land, say the Rosary with your families."

In his audiences he used to say, "Tell your friends that the Pope not only blessed your rosary, but that he says it every day himself.

"That is my last recommendation. **Say the Rosary.**" He himself died while saying the Rosary.

Leo XIII, deservedly called *"Lumen in Caelo,"* "Light of Heaven," recommended and preached the Rosary so earnestly when he became Pope that he was called the Pope of the Rosary.

He was already a very old man when he ascended the throne of St. Peter. It was a sad time for the Catholic Church. He was surrounded by bitter enemies, the Holy See was violently assailed and he himself was a prisoner in the Vatican.

Leo was a man of prodigious intellect, a profound philosopher, a consummate diplomat and a sagacious ruler.

Realizing the dangers that threatened him from every side, he placed all his confidence in the Rosary. Notwithstanding his unceasing labors and responsibilities, he found time to send a long series of magnificent encyclicals, which, year after year, he addressed to the whole world, to princes, bishops, to all the faithful, urging them to say the Rosary.

Though the month of May was consecrated to

Our Lady, he insisted that the month of October should be more especially consecrated to the Rosary and that the devotions should be carried out with great fervor and solemnity.

What was the result?

In a short time a truly wonderful change came about. His most powerful and bitter enemies not only ceased their hatred and persecution, but manifested for him the utmost respect and friendship.

Bismark, who had been cruelly persecuting the Church in Germany, made peace with Rome and went so far as to ask the Pope to act as arbiter between Germany and Spain in a grave dispute regarding doubtful territories claimed by both countries.

King Edward VII of England went himself on two occasions to Rome and paid royal honors to the Pope. He drove to the Vatican with every display of splendor and magnificence.

The Emperor of Germany rivalled the King of England in his manifestations of sympathy and respect.

Thus the sorrows of the Sovereign Pontiff were changed into joys, and his reign was one of the most glorious in the history of the Church.

When the venerable Pontiff lay on his deathbed, one of the Cardinals lovingly consoled him with the following words: "Remember, dear Holy Father, all you have done for the Rosary. God's Blessed Mother is waiting to take your soul to Heaven."

Pope Leo, though a profound philosopher, a

statesman of the highest standard, yet chose rather to place his confidence in the Rosary than in his own magnificent abilities.

Benedict XV declared the Rosary to be a most perfect prayer because of the immense joys and consolations it obtains, the enlightenment and divine knowledge it imparts and the triumphs and victories it wins for the Church, society, and the individual Christian.

Pius XI has added to the already immense number of indulgences which have won for the Rosary the title of the "Queen of Indulgenced Prayers."

He granted a Plenary Indulgence each time that anyone says the Rosary in the presence of the Blessed Sacrament, whether publicly exposed or enclosed in the Tabernacle.

BISHOPS AND SAINTS AND THE ROSARY

After the Roman Pontiffs, none have been so eager and zealous as the bishops of the world in their respective dioceses and priests in their parishes in preaching the Rosary.

When from some reason or other, after revolutions or persecutions, corruption and laxity had got hold of their people they had recourse to the Rosary, and with its help a complete regeneration in the minds and morals of their flocks became evident.

St. Charles Borromeo called the Rosary the most divine of devotions. He recited it daily on his knees. He ardently recommended it to his diocesans and made its recitation compulsory in colleges, seminaries and all pious institutions.

St. Francis de Sales had an implicit confidence in the Rosary from his earliest days and made a vow to recite it every day.

When he was engaged in the heaviest and gravest labors, fearing to forget the Rosary, he wound the beads around his arm to prevent such a possibility.

He always wore the rosary on his person and preached constantly on the necessity of saying it.

When, weak and exhausted, he could no longer articulate the words, he begged some of his assistants to say the prayers in a loud voice so that he could join with them, at least mentally.

He frequently urged St. Jane de Chantal never to miss saying the Rosary.

St. Alphonsus Liguori says that of all the devotions and prayers said in honor of Mary, he knows none to compare with the Rosary.

In his *Pastoral Theology* he recommended to all who have the care of souls to do their utmost to have the Rosary said.

Like St. Francis de Sales, he was so fearful of omitting his Rosary that he bound himself by vow to say it, and in his old age he begged his assistant brother never to allow him to forget his Rosary, because he said to him: "My eternal salvation depends on saying the Rosary."

EMINENT MEN AND THE ROSARY

Of the thousands of eminent men who have said faithfully their daily Rosary, we will mention just a few.

One of the most remarkable geniuses that the world has ever seen is Michelangelo, who was a painter, architect, poet and a genius of the very highest order.

This great man had a wonderful love for the Rosary. Among the many objects displayed in the Michelangelo Museum are two big rosary beads which he used so often. In his great fresco of the Judgment he depicts some of the souls with the rosary in their hands, trusting in its power to save them from Hell. His fervor in saying the Rosary in his last years was touching.

Then there was Clemens Brentano, the illustrious German poet and founder of a school of his own, whose devotion to the Rosary was no less extraordinary. He constantly recited it with the greatest faith.

Silvio Pellico, the famous Italian poet and writer, author of *Le mie prigioni, Francesca de Rimini,* etc., recited the Rosary every day.

Joseph Haydn, the great composer, looked upon as master and father by his colleagues, was once asked by a fellow musician how he found inspiration for his beautiful compositions. He replied, "When I feel dull I take up my rosary, and before I finish five Mysteries ideas crowd on me."

Gluck, the German composer, was intensely devoted to the Rosary—and so was Mozart.

DOCTORS

Some of the most famed physicians and surgeons of the world had a similar confidence in the power of the Rosary.

The celebrated Récamier surprised some of his less religious friends by his love for the Rosary. Once he said to them: "When I want to get an audience at Court, or even be received by one of our ministers, I experience much difficulty, and I have still more difficulty in obtaining what I ask for. But I have no difficulty in speaking to the Queen of Heaven, and I am always sure that she will hear me."

Laennec, who in his day was a man of mundane celebrity, not only said his Rosary, but loved to march in the Rosary processions. Once his carriage overturned and was damaged. While waiting for the needful repairs, he took out his rosary and began to pray.

Some of the nearby onlookers manifested their surprise, but Laennec said to them with a smile: "If I have experienced a bad accident, I have at least the right to enjoy the consolation of saying my Rosary."

Gautier de Ehlaubry had to accompany Napoleon's army to Spain. One day a band of infuriated Spaniards surrounded him in the streets of Madrid. No escape seemed possible. A happy thought struck him—he put his hand in his pocket and held up his rosary in the faces of the mob, who after a moment of hesitation allowed him to pass unmolested.

On his return to France, he told of this adventure and went publicly to church to give thanks to Our Lady of the Rosary for his escape.

The no-less distinguished Dr. Mooren of Dusseldorf said the Rosary daily, and more than once.

These are a few of the tens of thousands of great men who loved the Rosary.

In fact, the greatest minds find most delight and discover most beauty in this heavenly prayer.

THE HISTORY OF THE ROSARY

The history of the Rosary is one long story of wonders, favors, graces and blessings granted to all who say the Rosary.

How it began was thus: A ruthless sect of heretics sprang up in the south of France. Their doctrines were most pernicious, and their conduct barbarous in the extreme. Unfortunately, their numbers rapidly increased and their violence was manifested in burning churches, sacking towns, and murdering defenseless men and women who refused to accept their vile teachings.

Gradually they enrolled men of powerful influence in their ranks.

The Popes sent holy missionaries to try to convert them, but in vain. Kings sent armies against them, but to no purpose. Their excesses were such that they appeared to be demons let loose from Hell, rather than mortal men.

At this crisis St. Dominic appeared on the scene, but great saint though he was, he utterly failed to make an impression on them. They were so hardened that all he could do availed nothing.

In his difficulties, this great servant of God was always wont to appeal to Our Lady for help. Grave authorities, among them St. Antoninus, say that St. Dominic had during his life as many as a thousand visions of Our Lady. He himself confessed that she never refused him anything he asked.

She thrice solemnly declared that his Order was her own Order and gave his friars the white scapular which is the distinctive part of their holy habit.

To her the Saint now appealed with unbounded confidence. In answer to his prayer, she gave him the Rosary as a weapon by which he was to achieve the most extraordinary victories over evil.

In an incredibly short time he converted, by its help, one hundred thousand heretics, and this so effectively that many of them became very eminent for holiness.

That was the first great victory of the Rosary.

Since then thousands of the Saints, Blesseds, apostles and missionaries of the Dominican Order have spread this devotion through the length and breadth of Christendom.

But not only St. Dominic and his sons preached this prayer. Our Lady raised up saints at all times and in every country to preach and propagate it.

THE BATTLE OF LEPANTO

In the year 1571, the Turks had reached the zenith of their power. Christendom then seemed to be at their mercy.

Their armies were flushed with victory after victory. They were powerful, well-equipped and directed by the ablest generals. Their navy was far superior in every way to what the Christians could command.

The fairest provinces had fallen into their hands, and now their object was to capture France and Italy, seize Rome and transform St. Peter's into a Turkish mosque. St. Pius V then ruled the Church. This great Pontiff and Saint was appalled at the overwhelming danger that threatened the very ruin of Christian civilization.

The Christian powers were not only weak, but they were sadly divided among themselves. Intrigues, ambitions of power and personal animosities prevented that whole-hearted cooperation that was now so urgently necessary against their formidable foe.

The holy Pontiff put all his confidence in the Rosary, while at the same time he labored indefatigably to unite the Christian forces, such as they were. Finally he sent orders to them to put to sea—and though inferior to the Turks in number, in equipment, in artillery and in ships, they were to fight without fear, in the name of God and Our Lady.

On October 7, the two fleets approached each other.

To add to the difficulties of the Christians, the wind was against them, which in those days might have been a fatal disadvantage.

Obeying the orders of the Sovereign Pontiff and placing themselves under the protection of Mary, the Christian fleet dashed on the enemy with undaunted bravery.

Suddenly the wind, which had been so adverse, changed and blew violently in the face of the Turks and in favor of the Christians.

The battle raged with unabated fury for several hours, ending in the complete overthrow of the Turkish fleet.

The victory was so crushing and complete that the power of the Moslem was forever broken, and Christendom was saved.

During these terrible days and especially on the day of the battle, the Holy Father prayed fervently to Our Lady of the Rosary, marched in the processions, and exhorted the faithful to offer their Rosaries with intense fervor to the Mother of God.

At the moment of victory he fell into ecstasy, and it was revealed to him that the Christians had gained the day.

Turning to those around him, he gave them the news of the victory, and all fell on their knees and thanked God and His Blessed Mother.

We could multiply incidents like these a thousandfold.

LOURDES

Let us pause only to remember what Lourdes is, the monument erected to all the Christian world to Our Lady of the Rosary.

Not satisfied with raising up saints in every age and inspiring Popes, bishops and priests to preach the Rosary, the Mother of God came herself personally in our own days to preach the Rosary.

She appeared in Lourdes, and there her great message was: *"Pray the Rosary."* For this reason the Pope gave orders that the Basilica raised over the Grotto, by command of Our Lady, should be called the Basilica of the Rosary.

Countless multitudes of pilgrims flock annually from all parts of the known world to this hallowed spot to do honor to the Queen of the Rosary.

There the Rosary is the great prayer, there the *Aves* are heard unceasingly going up to the Mother of God, and there the gracious Queen of Heaven pours down on her children God's richest treasures.

Never since the time of Our Lord have prodigies been seen like those worked in Lourdes. The sorrowful and afflicted are consoled, sinners go away converted, the most extraordinary cures are wrought; the blind, the deaf, the dumb, the cripples are made whole.

Our sweet Lord Himself is pleased to honor His Blessed Mother, for some of the greatest of these miracles are worked at the blessing given by the most Holy Sacrament.

FATIMA

More recently still, in the year 1917, God's sweet Mother appeared once more, this time at Fatima, in Portugal, and here again her message was: *"Pray the Rosary."*

It is a glorious sight to see 300,000 men and

women of every age and class gathered on the hill-top of Fatima reciting, with the utmost faith and fervor, the Rosary.

In these few short years a marvelous change has come about all over Portugal, thanks to the Mother of God and the Rosary.

Portugal has sprung into a new and wonderful era of peace and prosperity. The faith of the people has revived miraculously, and a new and well-organized clergy is working zealously to bring back in all its ancient splendor the Faith that had made Portugal one of the greatest Catholic countries of the world.

Chapter 14

MEDITATIONS ON THE MYSTERIES

We are now about to deal with the most important element in the Rosary, namely, meditating on the Mysteries.

Unfortunately, many Catholics have little or no idea of how to meditate on the Mysteries. Therefore, for them the Rosary is not the Rosary. Instead of being a delightful prayer, it wearies them and they are glad when it is over.

In order to say the Rosary, one is bound to think on the Mysteries. This is the very essence of the Rosary and is what gives it its special charm and value.

The prayers, *viz.*, the Our Father, Hail Mary, and Glory Be to the Father are most precious, most efficacious prayers. It is impossible to form any just idea of the great graces we obtain by even a single Our Father, Hail Mary or Glory Be properly said, and nothing is easier than to say them properly. Nay, if said well, they give us incomparably more pleasure than if said badly. But—and this we can never stress sufficiently—the *soul* of the Rosary is the meditation of the Mysteries.

If one says the Our Fathers and Hail Marys and

does not think on the Mysteries, they doubtless get many graces—but they do not say the Rosary, they do not gain the indulgences of the Rosary and they do not gain the wondrous blessings promised to those who say the Rosary.

We must fully understand that it *is not difficult* to meditate on the Mysteries.

The word *meditate* frightens some people; they believe that it is difficult, and that they cannot meditate.

Perhaps the better and clearer word to use is *thinking* on the Mysteries.

It is easy for us to move our arms, our legs, to shut or open our eyes, to perform an act of any of our faculties.

But our most important faculties are our intellect, will, and imagination. With much more reason, then, can we use these great faculties; in fact, we are using them every moment of the day.

Boys and girls, men and women of every class are *thinking* about a thousand things every day, each in his own way.

That is all we are asked to do when saying the Rosary—to *think* on the Mysteries, but yet, as we shall see, this is all-important.

Each Mystery speaks to us of Our Lord, each teaches many beautiful lessons. Each one, too, reminds us of some duty or other that we have to perform. While thinking of the Mystery, or of the lessons it contains, we are praying to God and Our Lady to give us the graces necessary to do our duties, the light and help to understand what God is teaching us.

If we do this we gradually and, almost without knowing it, correct our faults and perform all our duties like good and true men. Above all, we begin to know and love God as we never knew Him before.

After all, the great reason why we are here on earth is to know God and serve Him, and save our souls. Life is of short duration. We may die any day. At the best we cannot live very long. But eternity lasts forever and ever, and will never, never end. Oh, for the happiness of Heaven!

The great end and object, then, of the Rosary is to teach us how to live well, how to be holy, how to be happy, and how to get to Heaven.

Another thing well worth remarking is that we cannot possibly be happy if we do not know and serve God.

Some foolish people think that to be holy and good means to be sad and austere. Nothing is more false. No one is so really, genuinely happy as the person who has God as his intimate, personal friend, in other words the person who is good and who knows God as He is. Is it hard to know God? Most certainly not. We have only to believe Him and recognize what He has done for us.

It is God, and only God, who can make us happy. Now that is exactly what the Rosary does for us. It makes us know God, know how good He is, makes us feel that He is our great, true Friend, our real Father, that no one more than He wishes us to be happy.

We will now explain briefly something about each Mystery.

When we say a Mystery, we first mention what it is, for example, the Annunciation or Visitation. Then we know what to think of and what to ask for as we recite the prayers.

Nothing can be easier, nothing more simple, and nothing more delightful.

THE JOYFUL MYSTERIES

The Joyful Mysteries put before our minds the great doctrine of the Incarnation in its various aspects, and each Mystery offers for our consideration a host of beautiful thoughts. To insure brevity and clearness we will confine our attention to a few of the more practical lessons, leaving our readers to meditate on any other points of doctrine that may suggest themselves.

Chapter 15

THE ANNUNCIATION

The story of this Mystery is as follows. God sent the Archangel Gabriel to announce to Mary that the hour so ardently longed for and prayed for by the Patriarchs, Prophets, and the holy ones of Israel had arrived.

The Word, the Son of God, was about to become man, and she was chosen to be His Mother.

The first thought, then, that presents itself to us is God made man for the love of us.

How little do many Christians know of this stupendous Mystery. Their thought when saying the first Joyful Mystery is, "The Angel announced to Mary that she is to be the Mother of God," and no more. Here they stop.

What good, we ask, can this vague thought do them, what food does it offer them for meditation?

What ought they to think of, what does the Incarnation really mean, what does the fact that *God became man* imply?

The Incarnation means everything for us; it means our eternal salvation, our happiness in this life, our happiness in eternity.

It is the greatest proof that God could possibly give us of His personal, intimate, infinite love for *each one* of us. God help us if we do not understand it and if we do not give ourselves the trouble of grasping it, feeling it, realizing it, for then God's great work will be of very little use to us.

What does this great act of God imply?

The Mystery is so sublime, so wonderful that not even the highest angel in Heaven could have dreamed of its possibility had not God revealed it.

St. Paul tells us that God emptied Himself out, that He exhausted all His infinite love, mercy, all His power and wisdom in becoming man for love of us. He the omnipotent Creator of Heaven and earth, He the God who fills the heavens with His majesty and glory, the Immense, Infinite, Eternal God reduced Himself to the weakness, the littleness of a tiny babe; He hid Himself for nine whole months in the womb of His Mother and was born in a stable between two animals. He then lived for 33 years in humility and poverty, subjected to countless insults and outrages, and finally died a most painful and ignominious death, crucified between two thieves!

We must not slur over these words; we must rather try and fathom their great meaning!

Remark, then, that God did all this not only for the human race in general, but for *each one* of us.

He saw me, He saw you, dear reader, and He did all He did for you and for me especially, as if we were the only beings in existence. This fact must fill our hearts to overflowing with love and consolation, but only if we stop to think of it, to feel it.

He became man and subjected Himself to all the

ignominies and sufferings of His Passion, not only to show us how much He loved us, but to compel and constrain us as far as He could, without destroying our liberty, to love Him. He not only loves us, but He most ardently desires that we love Him.

This is what He says Himself: "What could I do for My vineyard that I have not done?" What could I do to gain the love of men that I have not done? No, even God could do no more.

He not only became man and suffered and died for us, but He actually remains on all the altars of the world day and night for love of us.

He not only died once for us on the Cross, He dies for us every day on the altars, for in every Mass Jesus dies as really as He died on Calvary.

What oceans of love has not God poured out on us in the Incarnation. Why are we so cold, so insensible, so indifferent to this infinite love?

Simply because we do not pause to think, to understand this surpassing Mystery.

True, our poor minds are very weak, our hearts are cold and mean and the love of our God is infinite, immense.

How can we understand this infinite love of God?

By saying our Rosary daily. It enables us to drink in gradually, to absorb, to assimilate, to realize this Mystery of love.

Our minds are slow, but the Rosary puts before our eyes constantly and in the simplest way all our sweet Lord has done for us.

The crowds who flocked around Him when on earth were no more intelligent than we are—probably very much less cultured—yet they understood His goodness, they adored Him, they loved Him. So can we.

As we have already explained, while pondering on the Mysteries we are saying the Our Fathers and Hail Marys, two irresistible prayers, which obtain for us floods of divine light to understand and to feel.

Our sweet Lord asked the man in the Gospel: "Dost thou believe?" And he answered: "I believe Lord, help my unbelief."

Our thought, then, must be to believe all God has done for us, and our prayer to beg the Mother of God to give us this clear, vivid, and undoubting faith.

A second thought is suggested to us by the salutation of the Angel:

Bending low he said: *"Hail, full of grace."*

Mary had the plenitude of grace, grace sufficient, grace abundant to make her the worthy Mother of God, the peerless Queen of Angels. She has also grace sufficient, grace abundant to supply all the needs of her children. All graces come to us from God through Mary.

Mary disposes of all the treasures of her Divine Son. He refuses her nothing, so that St. Alphonsus says that she is in this way omnipotent.

On the other hand, she refuses us nothing. No mother of this earth ever loved a child, ever desired the happiness of her child as Mary loves us and desires our happiness.

In this Mystery, therefore, we must ask fervently for an abundance of divine grace. With this grace the weakest may become strong, and the vilest sinner can become a saint.

A third lesson we learn is from our dear Lady herself.

All the women of Judea had the ambition of one day becoming the Mother of God.

Only Mary never dreamed of this divine dignity.

She even made a vow of virginity, excluding herself, as she thought, from ever becoming a mother.

What a love for virginity, what profound humility!

Again, when the Angel assures her that by the omnipotent power of God she can be the Mother of God and remain a virgin, she accepts this divine honor with the utmost humility: "Behold the handmaid of the Lord." She who has been raised to the dignity of Mother of God, of spouse of the Holy Ghost, humbly and sincerely calls herself "the handmaid, the servant of the Lord."

Let us beg our dear Mother to obtain for us these two most precious gifts: purity and humility. With these two virtues we become most pleasing to God and are assured of His Divine love and affection.

When accepting the Divine Motherhood, Our Lady used a form which serves as another lesson for us. She did not say "I accept," but "Be it done to me according to thy word." She thus showed that it was not her will, but God's divine Will that she sought to do.

The highest perfection, the greatest happiness that we can attain is to wish to do only God's Will. Therefore we say every day: "Thy will be done." If we do the Will of God, we must be holy and happy. If we do not do the Will of God, we plunge ourselves into ruin.

Lastly, we would do well when saying this Mystery to offer to Our Lady all the joys and graces she received at the moment of the Annunciation and ask her for a great share of them.

(See page 37, The Hail Mary).

Chapter 16

THE VISITATION

The Second Joyful Mystery is the Visitation. The Blessed Mother of God hearing that her cousin, St. Elizabeth, needed her help started at once on a long and difficult journey to visit and console her.

Some Christians find little to meditate on in this Mystery, whereas the fact is that it contains a most important lesson for us all and teaches us a virtue that everyone is bound to practice as one of the essential duties and obligations of life.

The lesson God's Mother teaches us is charity, that virtue of virtues without which it is impossible for us to please God.

Our Lord assures us that whatever we do in favor of our neighbor He takes as done to Himself, and will give us the same reward as if we had done it to Him.

If we give even a cup of cold water to a poor man for love of God, we shall have an eternal reward. Do we realize this?

This virtue Our Lord calls His own: "This is **My** commandment that you love one another."

The early Christians practiced this virtue so carefully that the pagans in amazement used to exclaim: "See how they love one another."

Our Saviour tells us that when the just shall appear before Him in judgment He will say to them, "Blessed of My Father, come and receive what has been prepared for you from all eternity, for when I was hungry you gave Me to eat, when I was naked you clothed Me and when I was in prison you came to visit Me."

They will make answer and say: "But, dear Lord, we never had the opportunity to give You to eat and to drink."

He will then say: "But each time you did it to any of My little ones, to any of the poor, you did it to Me!"

And to the wicked He will say: "Begone, ye accursed of My Father. When I was hungry you did not give Me to eat, when I was thirsty you did not give Me to drink, when I was naked you did not clothe Me."

They will answer: "But Lord, we never knew You on earth, we never saw You." And He will say: "Every time you refused an alms to the poor, it was to Me you refused it."

Over and over again in the lives of the Saints, Our Lord shows us clearly that all we do to our neighbor we do to Him.

St. Martin gave half his cloak to a poor man, as he had nothing else just then that he could give. That night Jesus appeared to him in a vision, clad in that half cloak, and said: "Behold what Martin has given Me today."

Bl. Jordan of Saxony, when a student in the University of Bologna, was asked for an alms by a beggar. He had no money on his person so, with heroic charity, he undid a precious girdle that he wore and handed it to the suppliant. Some moments after, he entered a church to say a prayer before the great crucifix, when, to his surprise and delight, he saw his girdle around the waist of his crucified Lord! Jordan became a great saint and one of the greatest apostles of his time. He entered the Dominican order and succeeded St. Dominic as Master General.

We have countless opportunities every day of practicing this virtue.

We have the poor, to whom we may and should give generous alms. We have the souls in Purgatory, for whom it is our bounden duty to pray, and what can be more easy than to pray for these suffering souls. There are a thousand little acts of kindness which we can dispense to those around us. We can console and sympathize with those who suffer.

On the other hand, we are bound to refrain from censuring or criticizing others; we may not condemn or judge harshly the failings of those with whom we associate.

Yet, dear reader, no sin is more common than these failings in charity, and small though they may appear to be, these sins may hold us prisoners in Purgatory for long, long years.

The all-important subject of thought in this Mystery, then, is charity.

We must pray to God's dear Mother every time we think on the Visitation to obtain for us this virtue in an eminent degree.

She had just been made Mother of God. God was resting in her bosom as in a living tabernacle. Naturally, all her thoughts were for Him. Her ardent desire was to give herself to the most devout recollection, to the immense joys and delights of communing with her Divine Son. She was more intimately and lovingly united to Him than even the cherubs and seraphs who stand around His throne in Heaven.

Instead of yielding to these holy and legitimate inclinations, she at once undertook a dangerous journey in order to give the necessary succors to her cousin, St. Elizabeth, who was in need of her help.

What a sacrifice, what heroic charity! In those days roads were bad and much was to be feared from wild animals and robbers.

A second beautiful thought that this Mystery suggests is that we thank God for all the love and sweetness that He has bestowed on Mary. We are assured by the Saints that if we thank God for the virtues and graces He has given to any saint, we, thereby, receive a great share of those virtues.

Our Lord in His infinite mercy has made Mary the Queen of Mercy. He has made her our most loving and tender Mother. She is "our life, our sweetness and our hope." She is overflowing with compassion and pity for each of us. No sinner who has ever called on Mary has been abandoned. We must go to her in all our troubles, cares and sorrows, for no mother of this earth is so sweet and loving as she is.

We must, then, thank God with all our hearts for giving us such a dear Mother. We must ask Him to give us boundless trust in her, and we must thank and praise Him for all the wondrous graces He has given her.

Still another thought. Our Blessed Mother is so sweet, so loving, so kind. Let us ask her to give us a great share in her sweetness and gentleness.

Once a venerable priest said to the writer: "When I say the Second Mystery of the Rosary, I remind Our Blessed Lady that if St. Elizabeth was her cousin, I am her child, and that she helped and nursed St. Elizabeth. I ask her to help me and nurse me when I am sick and in trouble. As years are passing by and I feel that I am growing old, I ask her to look after me, not to abandon in my old age. And I am very sure that she will do all I ask her, so that I feel more easy in my mind."

He, too, asked Mary to obtain for him the grace to die on some day dedicated to her and to be with him at the hour of his death.

What a loving trust this dear old priest placed in his heavenly Mother! We all would do well to imitate him.

Chapter 17

THE BIRTH OF OUR LORD

This Mystery is truly a revelation of Divine Love.

We find ourselves in Bethlehem on Christmas night, looking on the Divine Infant lying on a bed of straw, warmed by the breath of two poor animals. And He is God!

We see Holy Mary bending over Jesus, her Son and her God, adoring, loving, blessing, thanking Him. What oceans of love fill her heart!

St. Joseph is filled with rapture that no words can describe. He is the adopted father, the protector, the defender of his God. He is actually taking the place of the Eternal Father in regard to Jesus.

There are throngs of angels singing their heavenly canticles. Here they are contemplating a vision of love that they had never seen in Heaven.

There they looked on the unveiled glory and majesty of the Godhead. Here they gaze on that same God, reduced for love of men to the form of an infant, wrapped in swaddling clothes and laid in a manger.

We behold the shepherds entering the cave, kneeling down and adoring their God. Of all the great ones of earth, these humble men were the first guests and friends that God invited to visit His Divine Son. A strange peace and joy and happiness fills their souls, a peace, a joy that they had never felt before.

And we! We assist at the self-same scene each time we hear Holy Mass. Jesus is really and as truly born on the altar as He was born in Bethlehem. Around the altar, around the priest are throngs of blessed spirits wrapt in contemplation. We are the guests, the friends whom God has specially invited to adore His Son.

Far more still, Jesus is born in our hearts in Holy Communion. He enters into our very souls. He embraces us, He loves us, He unites Himself most intimately to us.

As the water is united to the sponge which is immersed in it, as it is in its every particle, as the fire is in every pore of the iron placed in a furnace, so God is united to us most intimately in Holy Communion.

This is the thought, this is the meditation which we must make when saying this third Joyful Mystery.

Let us ask God's Blessed Mother to make us understand how Jesus is born on the altar at holy Mass, and how Jesus is born in our souls in Holy Communion.

Oh, if we had eyes to see and minds to understand, we should not be so cold, so distracted at Mass! Our hearts would burn with love if we only knew what Holy Communion means. The Churches would be thronged, and Catholics would flock in multitudes to the altar rails.

But all this will come to pass if we say our Rosary as we should, if we daily ask God's Mother to give us a lively, vivid faith in the great Mystery of the altar.

What was the difference between that one Communion which made Bl. Imelda a saint, and our Communions? Just this. She felt that her God was born in her heart. We do not.

If Zacheus, that hardened sinner, became a saint by one visit of our dear Lord, much more can we by one Holy Communion. Jesus entered the house of Zacheus, but He comes not into our *houses,* but into *our very souls.*

O Blessed Mother of God help us, help us to believe!

There is another thought that pleases Our Lady very much. It is this.

The happiest moment in a mother's life is when she holds her first-born baby in her arms and folds it to her heart. All her friends come to see her, to congratulate her. Her happiness is full.

Do we ever congratulate the Mother of God on that most blessed moment when Jesus was born, when she held Him in her arms and pressed Him to her heart?

If an earthly mother can feel such joy at the birth of her child, what must not God's dear Mother have felt at the birth of Jesus!

Let us then offer her anew this happiness, let us congratulate her, let us rejoice with her. She will be most grateful for this thought.

Why do not mothers of this earth, when saying this Mystery, beg and implore Mary—by her joy and happiness in becoming the Mother of God—to help them to rear their children well, to guard them from all evils.

Priests above all should ask Mary to help them at the dread moment of Consecration to say with infinite love: "This is My Body. This is . . . My Blood . . . for then Jesus is being born in their hands.

Chapter 18

THE PRESENTATION
IN THE TEMPLE

In this Mystery we consider how God's Immaculate Mother submitted herself to the Jewish Law of Purification—as though she who was so holy and pure required to be purified.

Moreover, she submitted her Divine Son to a similar humiliating ceremony.

Why? Simply to teach us by her example that fundamental lesson of our lives, *viz.,* our obligation to do our duty.

This is a simple and manifest principle, but one of unspeakable importance.

We expect the soldier to do his duty. If not, he is looked upon as a coward and poltroon.

We insist on our hired servants doing their duties. If they fail, we dismiss them.

The doctor who does his duty, whose whole heart is in his work, rapidly becomes an eminent practitioner. If he is remiss, he may cause the death of his patients.

The student who studies with great earnestness makes far more progress than his fellows, and he carves out an honorable and lucrative career. In contrast, the idler will likely, sooner or later, have to face poverty and disgrace.

The mother who instills into the minds of her children this golden rule gives to the world splendid men and women. If she neglects her duty, she is the cause of their unhappiness in life and very possibly of their eternal ruin.

It is the same in every branch of life. The person who invariably does his duty is happy, is successful and wins the esteem and confidence of everyone.

This is the first thought that must occupy our minds when saying the Fourth Joyful Mystery, *viz.,* to ask our Blessed Mother to give us a clear idea of the far-reaching importance of this great rule of life: "Do your duty, do it always."

There are occasions when it may be hard to do it, but if we are accustomed to do our duty in the small things of everyday life, then God will give us strength to do it under more difficult circumstances. When saying this Mystery, we must pray fervently for this essential virtue, the *love of duty,* the grace to do our duty on all occasions, fearlessly and unswervingly.

The Venerable Simeon and the Prophetess Anna watched daily for the coming of the Redeemer, and they received as a reward of their diligence the joy, the grace of being among the first of the children of Israel to see and adore the Messias.

Whoever, like them, does his duty, is no less certain of a great reward.

The thought of others when saying this Mystery is to ask for the grace of a happy death. When the aged Simeon received Our Lord into his arms, his heart overflowed with joy and peace, and he professed himself quite ready to die. We can never ask too frequently for this supreme grace of a holy and happy death.

There is still another important consideration that must not escape us. Simeon, looking on Mary, told her that a sword of grief would pierce her heart. We, too, must be prepared for sorrows and sufferings, for we are here in a land of exile; this is not our true home, it is a vale of tears. We are here to merit Heaven and its eternal rewards. All those many sufferings of life, the little ones and the great, are a source of infinite merit. We derive more benefit from five minutes of pain and sorrow patiently borne than from years of pleasure and success. Jesus, it is, who offers us a little share in His Passion. It is He who permits every pain and ache. With each cross, He gives a grace.

Therefore, we must offer all the annoyances and difficulties of life, sorrows, sickness and care, the irksomeness of work, all in union with the Passion and sufferings of Our Lord, in union with the dolors of our Blessed Mother.

Let us not forget to ask God's Mother to help us to bear our trials patiently. No one suffered as much as she did, Our Lord only excepted. No one knows better, no one is more ready to help and console us. Let us say often: "O dearest Mother, by that sword of sorrow that pierced your heart, help me to suffer!"

Not only the great sufferings of life, but also the small ones obtain for us merits and rewards exceedingly great. Do not let us lose these merits by our impatience. We can never repeat too often that the sorrows of life and, very especially, the small, daily ones will win us a crown like to that of the martyrs themselves **if patiently borne**.

It is well, too, to remember that when we bear pain patiently it loses all its sting, all its venom, and is relatively easy to bear.

When we are irritated or angry, then sorrow is intensified a hundredfold and becomes almost intolerable.

Chapter 19

THE FINDING OF JESUS IN THE TEMPLE

In the Fifth Mystery we think of how our Blessed Mother lost her Divine Son through no fault of hers, and how she found Him, after three days, in the Temple.

There are two considerations here: first, the bitter, poignant grief of Mary when she lost the Divine Child; second, her unspeakable joy upon finding Him.

Holy writers tell us that the loss of Jesus was one of Mary's greatest sorrows.

How different is our conduct when we lose Jesus! We lose God frequently, but we are so blind, so foolish that we do not feel our loss. We do not grieve over the separation from our God, we do not miss Him!

How do we lose God? First by sin. If our sin is mortal, we drive God from our souls and allow the devil to enter and take His place. Many Christians have not the faintest idea of the evil of mortal sin.

1) By it they lose God's friendship, God's love.

2) As long as they are in mortal sin, they are in open revolt against God.

3) No words can explain the awful filth and cor-

ruption of the soul in mortal sin. Were a man to see his soul in this state, he would die of horror.

4) At any moment he may die and fall into Hell. Hundreds and thousands are falling into Hell every day. A man in mortal sin is like a child walking on the edge of a precipice. He may in an instant fall headlong to an awful death.

Oh, dear reader, ask the Mother of God to preserve you and all dear to you from ever committing a mortal sin!

5) By a mortal sin you crucify the Son of God. By venial sins we also separate ourselves from God, but not to the same extent.

Sometimes a venial sin can be so grave that it is not easy to know whether it is venial or mortal. Secondly, a venial sin may detain us for long years in the dreadful fires of Purgatory, which St. Thomas says is the same fire as that of Hell. Such a sin must, indeed, be very grave if a merciful and loving God finds Himself obliged to punish it with such severity.

If a soul were to enter into the infinite joys of Heaven stained with only one venial sin, it would, of its own free will, abandon these great joys and plunge itself into the fires of Purgatory rather than remain with that single sin on its soul.

What, then, must we not think of the multitude of venial sins we so carelessly commit, our coldness, our indifference, our sloth, our tepidity, our excessive love of pleasure, our ingratitude, above all, our forgetfulness of God.

We do not allow God to enter into our lives, we do not know Him, we do not love Him as we ought.

We think about everything, but so little about God.

And yet God is our great friend—God and God alone can give us peace and joy and happiness.

The greatest evil in the world is to think that we can be happy without God.

The second consideration is the immense, unspeakable joy of Mary when she found Jesus.

Our most fervent prayer must be to ask God's Holy Mother by that immense joy she felt on finding her Divine Son to help us to find Him, too—that is, to know Him, to love Him, to trust Him, to treat Him as our friend.

This the Rosary will most certainly help us to do if we say it daily and fervently.

There is no grace that our Blessed Mother will more readily grant us than to help us to know and love her Divine Son.

WHY SHOULD WE LOVE GOD?

Here are nine reasons:

God is infinitely good and lovable. Were we to see Him for one moment, our hearts would burn with love for Him and we should fly to Him.

It is the sight of God's beauty and love and mercy that fills Heaven with happiness. This is the God that we are asked to love.

If the devil could see God for one instant, his being would be so filled with happiness that he could never suffer again.

God made us with infinite love.

God died the awful death of Calvary for the love of us.

God made our hearts expressly and solely to love Him, and they can never be happy if they do not love Him.

The smallest act of love will have an eternal reward.

The greatest works a man can do, if they are not done for the love of God, are worth nothing.

The heart of man that was made for God can never rest or find peace or be happy if it does not love God.

This, then, is the grace we must ask Our Lady in the Fifth Joyful Mystery: to find God, to know God and to love God.

Chapter 20

THE SORROWFUL MYSTERIES

The Sorrowful Mysteries of the Rosary obtain for us the ineffable grace of understanding the Passion of Our Lord.

We can never repeat too often that Jesus underwent the awful ignominies and sufferings of the Passion simply to win our love. He could have saved us by one word, by one drop of His Precious Blood. Why, then, did He undergo the insults, the mockery, the unspeakably cruel pains of His Passion? It was to prove to us how much He loves us.

If we do not *realize* all He suffered, we are defeating the principal end of His greatest work, His greatest proof of love, the Passion.

Yet many understand little of the Passion. Their hearts are as cold as ice—they are utterly unmoved by the sight of the Crucifix, or by hearing the story of the Passion. It would appear as if it were all a legend, rather than a reality.

Every word and act of Our Lord during His life was meant to be a lesson for us. The greatest, the most astounding act in all His life was His Passion. It is, then, the lesson of lessons for each one of us.

Ask yourself, dear reader, if you feel, if you realize, if you grasp the magnitude of God's love for you in the Passion.

In a word, is the Passion the great, living reality of your life? Do you really believe that Jesus died for you? If so, why do you not love Him?

The Saints and holy Doctors tell us that five minutes spent in prayer and meditation on the Passion is worth hours and hours spent in other devotions. Nay, they say that one tear shed in sympathy and sorrow for the sufferings of Our Lord may obtain pardon for all our sins.*

All the saints, St. Alphonsus teaches, became saints because they loved to think on the Passion of Our Lord, and no saint became a saint without deep devotion to this holy Mystery.

How comes it then that so many, who call themselves friends of Our Lord, think so little of the sufferings He underwent for *them.*

Once more, the Rosary comes to our help and guarantees us a real understanding of Our Lord's Passion if we say the Sorrowful Mysteries devoutly and intelligently. No one need fear that it is above their powers.

We saw in the story of the old Irish woman how deeply and truly she felt the sorrows of her Lord.

Like her, let us kiss our crucifix each time we say the Rosary, lovingly and affectionately, with the intention of offering our sweet Lord the love and sorrow of His Mother when she stood at the foot of the Cross and when she received the torn

---

* This should be understood in light of the Church's teaching on Perfect Contrition.

and mangled body of Jesus into her arms, and tenderly kissed His five Wounds.

O Blessed Mother of God, help us to *feel* the sufferings of your Jesus and your own most bitter dolors!

Nothing will give Our Lord so much pleasure as our honoring His Passion. He will give us readily and abundantly the grace to understand it *if we ask Him*.

No prayer, no penance will wipe out our sins as efficaciously as meditating on the sorrows of Our Lord.

Let us have the wish to apply all the infinite merits of the Passion and Precious Blood to our souls when we say these Mysteries. Let us, too, offer all our troubles in union with and for love of Jesus Crucified.

Chapter 21

THE AGONY OF JESUS
IN THE GARDEN

Our Lord, the Son of God, enters the Garden of Olives.

His soul is **sorrowful unto death.**

What sorrow, what anguish must it not have been that wrung this confession from the Son of God.

He enters the Garden, He actually asks His weak disciples to help Him, to watch with Him. To what straits is He not reduced when He thus solicits the consolation of weak men.

In the darkness of the night He sends up that heartrending cry to His Eternal Father: "Father, Father, if it be possible let this chalice pass from Me, yet not My will, but Thine be done."

He accepts the chalice and drinks it to the dregs.

Then He falls on His knees in an agony of infinite desolation. His precious blood bursts from every pore of His sacred body in the extremity of His anguish.

Why all this? Our sins—your sins, dear reader, and mine.

What is it that He sees? The vision, the awful vision of all He has to suffer, in its every detail.

What is incomparably worse, He sees all the hideous sins and crimes of men. He who is holiness itself takes upon Himself all the malice and wickedness of mankind. No wonder that the blood pours out from every pore in His sacred body.

He sees the black ingratitude of men. He sees the countless millions of souls who, notwithstanding all His sufferings, will in their foolishness and madness, hurl themselves into Hell by their deliberate sins.

Would that we could feel the infinite truth, the reality of Christ's agony, and above all that we could feel that He, the Son of God, did all this for me and for you.

Let us beg and pray and implore our Blessed Mother to help us to understand this infinite love. Let us offer the blood, the anguish, the infinite merits of Christ's Agony in the Garden in atonement for our sins. Let us offer His detestation for sin, His sorrow, to make up for our want of sorrow and repentance.

He offered all this for me. His sufferings are mine. Let me offer them in union with the Masses being said all over the world to obtain pardon for my sins and pardon for the sins of the world.

It is well to say this first Mystery before going to Confession. Many have grave doubts as to the sincerity of their sorrow. Let them say this Mystery devoutly.

Chapter 22

THE SCOURGING AT THE PILLAR

In this Mystery, we contemplate the incomprehensible fact of a God being barbarously scourged by His enemies in a public square before a savage mob, a mob of His chosen people, whom He came to save!

The details of this scourging are impossible to describe. We will mention the main facts.

Christ was stripped of His garments and bound to a pillar. The fiercest executioners that His enemies could find were armed with dreadful scourges, and several of these barbarians at a time showered blows with horrible savagery on the delicate body of our Saviour. When one group of them seemed exhausted, fresh ones took their places, and for one awful hour these inhuman monsters—with all the strength of their brawny arms dealt no less than 6,000 blows on the Christ God. His body was a mass of hideous wounds, from the crown of His head to the soles of His feet.

Oh, what agony! How did He live through it? He was borne up by His omnipotent love.

Why, dear Lord, did You suffer this indescribable suffering? For me, for my sins! I believe it.

Can there be any doubt? No, none whatever. Sweet Lord, as blow after blow fell on Your poor, defenseless flesh You saw me, You offered every pang of those awful tortures for me, and why? To satisfy for my self-love, my sensuality, my sensuousness, my want of chastity and purity, the sinful indulgence of my passions.

Blessed Mother of God, who looked on that awful sight, ask your Divine Son to apply to my poor soul the merits of that awful scourging. But O, Sweet Mother, ask Him even more to make me see and feel and understand His love for me.

We should do well to offer this Mystery, too, in penance for our sins, to make up for all our want of mortification, our self-love, our idleness, our self-indulgence.

Let us ever bear in mind that the application of the Passion to our souls is incomparably more meritorious than the severest mortification.

Chapter 23

THE CROWNING WITH THORNS

Our Lord crowned with thorns.

The enemies of Our Lord, in their insensate fury, invented unheard-of tortures for the innocent Son of God.

In diabolical derision they resolved to crown Him as a mock king with a crown of long, sharp, piercing thorns. They wove this crown in such fashion that the thorns entered the head from every angle.

We must remember that Our Lord's body was especially sensitive, so that Jesus suffered with an intensity of which we can form no idea.

The soldiers pressed the crown on our Saviour's head with brutal force. The thorns were driven deeply into the head and came out in the forehead and cheeks. Moreover, they struck His head violently, and several times tore off the crown, dragging out the thorns, and then replaced it with renewed brutality.

St. Anselm says that the thorns were as many as 72, but the horrible wounds inflicted by them were fully a thousand. The unutterable agony of this torture lasted until Our Lord's death, so that the divine head was literally racked with the most intense pain.

Far from showing the slightest pity, the soldiers and executioners, egged on by the Jews, insulted, blasphemed, and made a mockery of Christ.

Again let us remember that Jesus was really the Son of God, the great Creator and omnipotent Lord of Heaven and earth.

Why did He submit to this blasphemy, this derision, this excruciating torture?

He did it for the love of you, for the love of me; He did it to win, to compel our love. Is it not an awful crime, the most black ingratitude, outrageous folly on our part not to give ourselves the trouble to understand this infinite love of Our Lord for us?

When saying this Mystery, we must pray most earnestly to God's Blessed Mother to obtain for us the grace to realize and comprehend, in all their clearness, these new sufferings of Jesus for us. We must ask her to awaken in our cold, indifferent hearts a corresponding love, gratitude and recognition of this divine love.

Let us ask Our Lord for the grace, too, to bear patiently for love of Him the insults and offenses that we may have to face during our poor lives.

But God has another equally loving motive in suffering so cruelly. He wished to make the fullest atonement for the countless sins which we might call *of our heads,* that is the foolish, wicked, selfish, vile thoughts with which we have so often and so gravely offended Him. Our minds are imitations of the divine mind. Our intelligence is our highest and noblest faculty, by which we are made like to God Himself.

The thoughts that flow through this intelligence should be worthy of God. Yet how often, how constantly, we harbor wicked thoughts, thoughts of pride, vanity, self-love, thoughts of anger and bitterness, thoughts of impurity which defile our souls and make them filthy and corrupt, like to the devil himself.

Then there are the multitudes of foolish, useless thoughts, thoughts of impatience and unrest, useless fears and doubts.

Every one of the thousands and thousands of thoughts that pass through our minds might so easily be an act of perfect love, as we explained when speaking of the Morning Offering.

In this Mystery let us apply the infinite merits of the Crowning of Thorns to our souls, to our minds. Let us beg God to forgive all the innumerable, sinful and useless thoughts of the past, and grant us the grace to use our minds and imaginations in the future for His glory and for our own benefit and happiness.

PRAYER

O Jesus, by the indescribable pains which You suffered in the Crowning of Thorns, pardon the countless sins which we have committed by bad thoughts and imaginings! Amen.

Let us ask for that precious virtue of humility which will give us that peace which we all so much desire.

Chapter 24

CHRIST CARRYING HIS CROSS

In the Fourth Sorrowful Mystery, we contemplate Christ carrying His Cross to Calvary.

At a glance we see the innumerable thoughts this Mystery offers us. We are familiar with the Way of the Cross, with its fourteen stations.

This Mystery of the Rosary puts before our minds all these fourteen considerations.

It is not always easy for us to go to the church and make the Stations, but it is very easy for us to say the Fourth Sorrowful Mystery of the Rosary. Unhappily, some people say this Mystery and derive little of the immense benefit they might derive from it.

Christ carrying His Cross, Christ the Son of God, equal to the Father and Holy Ghost, utterly exhausted by the suffering and loss of blood shed first in the Agony and secondly in the scourging at the pillar. Six thousand awful lashes were showered on His body; every lash opened a gaping wound and caused a copious flow of blood. Then came the Crowning of Thorns with its excruciating and prolonged agony.

Though suffering from extreme exhaustion,

with His body covered with wounds, His head racked with pains, His soul filled with anguish and desolation, He is obliged to carry that heavy Cross.

Its sharp edge has worn an awful wound in His right shoulder, which of itself causes Him intense pain.

Time after time, utterly worn out, He falls on the rough rocks and stones, and the weight of the Cross crushes Him to the earth, opening again His wounds and causing a fresh flow of the little blood left in His worn-out body.

Instead of help and pity, kicks and blows are showered on Him; He is insulted and blasphemed.

Oh, how His Blessed Mother's heart is rent with grief! She cannot help, she cannot console Him.

Again we ask ourselves the question, why did God suffer these fresh outrages, this contumely, these insults?

We make answer, He did all this for love of us, to obtain pardon for our sins, to save us from Hell, above all, to constrain us to love Him.

Why are we so hard, so cold, so ungrateful, so unbelieving?

O Mother of Jesus, make us believe, open our eyes, make us see how God loves us!

If we might ask, what had our dear Lord especially in view when He made the Way of the Cross? It was this:

He saw our miserable weakness, He saw our daily falls, our miseries, our sins, our helplessness.

He suffered the dreadful pains of the Way of the Cross to merit strength for us, strength to arise from the mire in which we wallow, strength to overcome the miserable vanities that beset us, strength to be men, strength to be sons of God.

Once more we call your attention, dear readers, to this **outstanding fact,** *viz.,* that all God's efforts, all His sufferings, all the graces He offers us are well nigh lost on us if we do not take the trouble to think on them, to understand them.

Many do so, and these are a thousand times blessed.

Jesus on the Cross did all He could to save the two thieves who were crucified by His side. He prayed for them. He offered personally His sufferings for them.

One remained deaf to all His efforts and was lost. The other accepted the grace our sweet Lord offered him, and he had the happiness to hear: "This day wilt thou be with Me in Paradise."

So it is happening every day. Some listen to the pleadings of God, some accept His grace, and these will be with Him forever in Heaven.

Others go on trifling with God, and are lost forever!

In this Mystery, let us ask Our Divine Lord, by His dreadful falls on the way to Calvary, to give us strength to fall no more, or at least not to fall gravely, not to fall so often.

Let us pity and compassionate God's dear

Mother, in the agony of sorrow which rent her heart on seeing the sufferings of her Son.

Let us offer Jesus the sympathy, the compassion, the sorrow of His Holy Mother when she met Him carrying His Cross.

Let us offer Him the towel of that heroic woman, St. Veronica, with which He wiped His adorable face.

Finally, let us offer Him the compassion and sympathy of the holy women of Jerusalem who fearlessly offered Him the expression of their deep grief, their horror on seeing His suffering.

If we say this Fourth Sorrowful Mystery devoutly, God will give us abundant strength to carry our crosses during life.

Chapter 25

JESUS DIES ON THE CROSS

The Fifth Sorrowful Mystery is the Crucifixion and death of Jesus Christ.

It is incredible how little many Christians feel Christ's death. It is for them a fact like a thousand other facts, but it has little or no appeal for them.

If a friend does us a small favor, much more if he does us a great favor, we have no words to thank him. We long for an opportunity to repay him, or at least to show our gratitude.

On the other hand, how many Christians never thank God for having suffered and died for them! Ask yourself, dear reader, how often have you thanked God, the great God of Heaven and earth, for having been crucified for you. And if you have thanked Him, how cold, how unfeeling was not your thanks.

Not only has He given you the greatest, the most personal proof of His love by dying for you, He has saved you from Hell, He has given you the most abundant graces and blessings. Notwithstanding that, you repay Him so little for this love.

Jesus has at last arrived on the summit of Mount Calvary.

His executioners rush on Him, they tear off His garments, and with them they tear off pieces of His bleeding flesh. What a sight that Sacred Body presented to His poor Mother!

Then they threw Him on the Cross, which was so badly prepared that they caused Him new and excruciating torture by the savage violence with which they dragged His hands and feet to the holes made for the nails.

His Blessed Mother heard the awful blows which drove the great, rough nails through His hands and feet into the wood of the Cross.

In the meantime a deep hole was dug, and the executioners lifted the Cross on high and dropped it into this pit which was prepared for it. As the Cross fell, the whole body of Our Lord, which was hanging from four nails, was racked with the most intense pain caused by the shock of the Cross as it fell into its place.

The Jews scoffed, mocked and blasphemed Him.

The soul of Christ was filled with infinite sorrow and desolation so that He cried out in His anguish: "My God, My God, why hast Thou abandoned Me?"

In the Garden of Olives He cried out, **"Father, Father,** if it be possible let this chalice pass from Me."

On the Cross He cried out, "My God, My God, why hast Thou abandoned Me?"

No words could describe more eloquently the grief, the desolation which He felt during those three dreadful hours on the Cross.

The Eternal Father gazed on the awful sufferings of His Divine Son. It was He who sent Him to save sinful and ungrateful man.

The angels in Heaven contemplated the God of Majesty, amazed at such infinite goodness.

Mary stood by the side of the Cross, the Queen of Sorrows, the Queen of Martyrs.

She was holier than all angels and men, and she suffered in proportion to her sanctity. She suffered with her Divine Son, she cooperated with Him in our redemption.

Let us ask her to engrave on our minds, on our hearts **the truth** that God really died for us.

Chapter 26

A LOVER OF THE PASSION

There lived in the beautiful old Dominican Convent of Ulm a white-robed sister who was a universal favorite with the members of the community. She was always cheerful, always gay, ever dispensing loving smiles and kind acts to all around her. No one was more devout, no one more obedient.

Among her devotions, a love for the Passion of Our Lord held a special place in her heart.

In the cloister leading to the choir stood a large crucifix, at the foot of which Sr. Mary loved to kneel and gaze up at the face of her crucified Lord.

The sisters, as they passed in their visits to the choir, glanced affectionately at their little Lady of Dolors.

As time went on, her sweet young face assumed an expression of pain. Then her visits to the crucifix grew fewer, and finally ceased altogether.

The sisters, who loved her dearly, were surprised all the more, as they remarked that now, instead of kneeling, as had been her wont at the foot of the Cross, she hastened past it with head averted.

When the venerable Provincial called to see the community, he asked as usual for the sisters.

The Mother Prioress, fearing that the little sister was suffering from scruples or some dangerous illusion, mentioned the change that she had remarked in her behavior.

The good Father bethought him of a plan to remove all doubts. He gathered the sisters around the great crucifix and made a touching discourse on the sufferings of Our Lord. From time to time he glanced at Sr. Mary, and in truth he noted an expression of deep grief on her face. He concluded his conference with some consoling and comforting words, assuring the sisters of the great affection that Jesus bears for those who love His Passion and who venerate His Sacred Wounds.

He then knelt at the foot of the Crucifix and kissed the feet of the Christ, asking the sisters to do as he had done.

All gladly obeyed until it came to the turn of Sr. Mary, who hesitated for a moment and then, throwing herself onto her knees, cast one swift glance at the face of Jesus, kissed His sacred feet, and uttering a cry of anguish, fell lifeless on the floor.

Filled with grief and consternation, they lifted her gently and placed her on her couch.

A holy priest, with whom the little sister sometimes took counsel, hearing of what had happened came in haste, and seeing the sorrow of the aged Provincial sought to comfort him. "She has died of love, dear Father, I do assure you," he said. "At first her devotion to the Passion was like that of all of us, but gradually, by frequent meditation on

Christ's sufferings and by earnest prayer to God to make her know and feel His love even as the Saints had felt it, she came to have so vivid a comprehension of this great Mystery that no longer—because of the bitter anguish that filled her heart—could she look on that divine face which she loved so tenderly.

"Be certain, Reverend Father, that Sr. Mary has died of love for the Crucified."

This beautiful fact teaches us that though at first we may feel cold and indifferent at the sight of all that God suffered for us, yet if we continue to ponder and think on the Passion, and if, above all, we ask God to make us understand His great love, we too shall obtain a deep devotion and tenderness for this Mystery of Mysteries.

When saying the Sorrowful Mysteries, let this be our aim.

THE MONK'S VISION

In an Eastern monastery held in high repute for the sanctity of its members, Br. Palemon was the most conspicuous of all for his many virtues. He had, however, one difficulty. He was sprung from a lordly stock, and in his youth he had been reared in luxury. The bread of the monastery was black and sour, and the good monk never quite overcame his repugnance to its unsavory taste.

Our Blessed Lord, well pleased at his noble endeavors to reach perfection, appeared to him one night in a vision, bearing His Cross on the way to Calvary and surrounded by His cruel and relentless enemies, who heaped insults and out-rages on Him.

Palemon sprang to the side of his Saviour and boldly sought to help Him to carry His Cross.

Jesus looked on him with love and said: "How can you bear this heavy Cross when you find it so hard to eat the bread of the monastery?" Then, giving him a loaf of the black bread on which some drops of His Precious Blood had fallen, He bade him eat.

Never did Palemon eat anything so delicious.

The vision passed, but henceforth the memory of the awful sufferings of his Lord made all things easy to Palemon, and the easiest and most con-soling of all was the eating of the bread of the monastery, which he softened with the tears he shed at the thought of his Lord's sufferings.

It will be easy for us to bear our sufferings in patience if we only offer them in union with Christ's bitter Passion.

DEVOTION TO OUR LADY'S DOLORS

In the time of St. Bridget a rich man lived in Sweden, who unfortunately gave unrestrained license to his passions. For fifty and more years he had never confessed, never received Communion. He gave much scandal in the town in which he lived. He at last fell mortally ill, and obstinately refused to repent.

Our Lord made it known to St. Bridget that she must send her confessor to the bedside of the dying sinner. She did so, but in vain. The unfortunate man persistently refused to make his peace with God, saying that after such a life of sin and iniquity there could be no hope, no pardon possible for him.

Once more Our Lord bade the Saint send her confessor, who was to tell the dying man that he was sent by God Himself.

The Saint, marveling much at this extraordinary mercy of God, did as she was commanded.

This time the good priest, after many efforts and after telling the sick man that he had come by the orders of the Almighty, succeeded in converting him. After some days he died, sincerely repentant.

When Jesus once more appeared to St. Bridget, she humbly asked Him why it was that He showed such infinite mercy to that unhappy sinner.

Our Lord revealed to His holy servant that He did so because, in the midst of all his disorders, the rich man ever showed a great love and compassion for His Blessed Mother's sorrows.

From this we see how meritorious is devotion to Our Lady's dolors.

When saying the Sorrowful Mysteries, we should not fail to think, too, on the bitter tears, the anguish that God's Holy Mother suffered on Calvary.

Chapter 27

THE RESURRECTION

The Resurrection is the greatest feast of the Church because it commemorates the triumph of God over His enemies, over sin and over the devil.

St. Paul says that if Christ had not risen, our faith would be in vain.

Christ wrought wonderful miracles during His life, proving clearly that He was the Son of God, but He promised the greatest miracle of all after His death, namely, the Resurrection, as the *special proof* of His divinity.

The Jews understood this full well, so much so that they asked Pilate for a body of soldiers to guard the Holy Sepulchre, for they said: "This imposter has said that on the third day He will rise from the dead. Lest then His disciples come and steal away His body and say that He has arisen, set a guard at the tomb."

When Our Lord, as He had foretold, did actually arise, they sought to deny the Resurrection, but in vain. Their efforts only served to prove more clearly the fact that He had arisen and that He was indeed the Son of God.

Our Lord was born and lived for each one of us, He suffered and died for each one, and so He rose from the dead for each of us.

We marvel at some of those acts of personal love He has given to saints, proofs of love for which they could never thank Him sufficiently, even though they lived a thousand years.

Why cannot we understand what Our Lord has done for us, 1) *by becoming man* expressly for each one of us; 2) *by dying on the Cross* for each one; and 3) *by rising from the dead* for each one.

We have already accentuated this fact, but if we repeated it many hundreds of times it would be little, if only we could convince you, dear reader, if we could make you feel its truth.

God has lived, died and risen for us—all stupendous Mysteries of love. More, He has made over to us the infinite merits of His life, death and Resurrection. He has given them to us, and we can offer them to Him as our very own property!

Therefore, when saying this Mystery we must ask God, by the infinite merits of the Resurrection, to give us grace to triumph over death, over sin and over the devil.

Another and very useful thought is to ask God for health of mind, health of body. He triumphed over death — let us ask Him by His infinite merits to give us health of body.

Did He not give health to the sick, sight to the blind and movement to the paralytic when He was on earth?

Does He not do so constantly at Lourdes? Does

He not give His saints and holy ones power to restore us to health when doctors and all human means have failed. The priest, at the most solemn moment of Holy Mass, when he holds his God in his hands, asks for this very grace. Is not fervent prayer obtaining health every day for those who ask it?

Let us then offer Him the merits of His Resurrection and ask Him to give us health, if it be His holy will.

A third thought. Jesus in His Resurrection triumphed over sin.

Let us ask Him, full of confidence, to pardon all our sins, to give us strength to conquer all temptations.

A fourth thought is that Easter is the feast of joy, of alleluias. On Easter morn, Heaven and earth resound with alleluias of praise, joy and exultation.

Let us ask God to give us the great grace of joy and peace and confidence.

Many foolishly worry themselves all their lives with useless cares and fears; they wear around their necks, as it were, a heavy weight of sadness.

Let us pray with all our hearts to God's sweet Mother and ask her by the transports of joy she felt on Easter morn on beholding her Divine Son, glorious and triumphant, to give us a share of her joy. She is our sweet Mother, and she will surely give it to us.

As St. Paul says, the Resurrection is the feast of our faith, it is the basis and ground of faith. Had Christ not arisen, our faith would be in vain.

Therefore, we must ask in this Mystery, above all other graces, for a clear, a vivid, a strong and an ardent faith.

Had we faith, we could move mountains. Had we faith, we could see all the beauty and consolation of our holy religion.

Chapter 28

THE ASCENSION

In this Mystery we contemplate the delight and joy of the Blessed Virgin, the Apostles and the disciples on seeing the Divine Master going up to Heaven, resplendent with glory.

Many beautiful thoughts suggest themselves when reciting this Second Glorious Mystery.

First of all, we should rejoice with all our hearts, as the Apostles did, on seeing this new triumph of Our Lord. We have followed Him in His sorrows— it is fitting that we take part with Him in His joys.

A second thought is that though the Apostles were sad and fearful at the thought of separation from their loved Master, for not only did their poor hearts burn with love of Him, but they felt their own weakness, alas, only too well. What were they to do when the Master was gone? To whom have recourse? From whom ask for help? He had been everything to them.

Yet, after the Ascension they returned to Jerusalem rejoicing. Why?

Our Lord had promised them that though He

was going up to Heaven, He would ever be with them and be with us, too, until the end of time.

OUR LORD IS WITH US IN DIFFERENT WAYS

He is with us by His divine presence and Providence. Not a hair falls from our heads without His permission. Nothing happens to us without His consent. He is ready to assist us in our every difficulty, danger and sorrow, if only we call on Him: "Jesus save me, Jesus help me."

This is indeed a truth of transcendent importance, that our dear Lord is ever present to us, ever ready to comfort and console us; a truth that we must grave deeply in our hearts and hold every day and every moment before our eyes.

God never permits a sorrow to overtake us that He does not give us a mighty grace and strength to bear.

But we must think of Him, we must call on Him, we must trust Him. Happy, a thousand times happy are those who realize the presence of God, who place their trust in Him.

GOD IS WITH US IN THE BLESSED SACRAMENT

How few of us enjoy Our Lord's Presence as we should. How few of us drink of the living waters that He dispenses to those who visit Him in His Sacrament of love. What delights we might enjoy at the foot of the altar!

We must pray most fervently to our sweet Mother to give us a vivid, living faith in this

Divine Sacrament.

Is God really there on the altar? Does He really see me and hear me? Does He love me but with a personal love?

Oh, surely, most certainly He does! Just to think of it, we may go into the very Presence of our God any moment we like! He is there on the altar waiting for us, longing for our visits, ready to fill our souls with the most precious graces.

How can men and women be so utterly blind as not to visit Our Lord frequently and lovingly in the church?

St. Aloysius' love for Our Lord in the Blessed Sacrament was so intense, his visits so frequent that the doctors thought it well to discontinue, or at least to lessen these visits, for his health was very weak.

As a consequence, his superiors ordered him to go less frequently, to pray less intensely before the altar.

The dear Saint confessed that this was the only time that he felt it hard to obey. His heart so burned with love for Jesus on the altar that he found it hard to resist the call of this burning love.

St. Dominic, after the most arduous labors of the day, sought as his only recompense the pleasure of passing the night with Jesus in the Blessed Sacrament.

St. Thomas Aquinas enjoyed the intensest pleasure before the altar. He spent whole nights in raptures of love.

We could fill books and books with such like acts of faith and love.

One may say: These were saints!

It is not necessary to be a saint to know and feel that Jesus is in the Blessed Sacrament.

All we need do is to think and pray, to ask God to open our poor, blind eyes.

The Countess of Ferrari passed hours and hours before the Blessed Sacrament.

Protestants themselves feel the need, the urge to visit Jesus on the altar.

A Protestant minister was accustomed to go to a Catholic church in Ireland on days when the Blessed Sacrament was exposed. On leaving he used to say: "Oh, blessed faith of you Catholics who can visit and talk to your God so easily."

An atheist once said: "If I could believe that my God was on the altar, I should never wish to leave the church."

A friend thus writes from New York City: "I expected to see wonders in this great city, and I certainly was not disappointed; but what I least expected to find surprised me most. Strolling down one of the great thoroughfares in the late afternoon, just as the innumerable offices of the city were closing for the day, I saw crowds of eager, active, bustling men of all ages pouring into the streets on their way home. I remarked with no little surprise that very many paused at the church door and entered. Curious to know what this meant I, too, went in. I found the sacred edifice filled. All were on their knees, some with eyes earnestly fixed on the Tabernacle and lips moving in silent prayer, others with heads bent down in rapt devotion. They remained thus for a few minutes, then left. The church again filled rapidly, and the same scene was enacted anew. I was amazed. In this great Babylon, where to live is to struggle, where time is money, it is indeed touching to see such a grand, daily act of faith in the Blessed Sacrament."

Jesus is with us, too, by devotion to His Sacred Heart. The best and easiest way to practice this devotion is:

1) to place a picture of the Sacred Heart in our rooms.

2) to repeat frequently during the day these few words, "Sacred Heart of Jesus, I place my trust in Thee."

3) to wear a badge of the Sacred Heart.

4) to make the nine First Fridays.

Chapter 29

THE DESCENT
OF THE HOLY GHOST

The Third Glorious Mystery has a most important and consoling lesson for us all.

Our Lord had chosen for His Apostles weak, ignorant and timid men, yet these were destined to convert not a people, not a nation, but the whole world, a world sunk in vice and depravity. He chose weak men for this mighty work, to teach us that the weakest man, by the aid of His grace, can do all things.

After the Ascension of Our Lord, the Apostles were gathered together in company with God's sweet Mother, preparing themselves for the coming of the Holy Ghost, whom Jesus had promised to send.

The Apostles were still weak and timid, afraid of the Jews and far from understanding all the heavenly doctrine Our Lord had taught them.

On the tenth day the Holy Spirit descended on them in the form of tongues of fire, and sat on the heads of each one of them.

In a moment these simple, ignorant, timid men were filled with the wisdom and strength of God. Their weakness gave way to an amazing strength, their fears were dispelled and their blindness was illuminated by the lights of God's Spirit to such an extent that they fearlessly entered the Temple and synagogues and preached Christ Crucified with clearness and eloquence that convinced and converted thousands of their listeners.

They discoursed in the presence of their enemies, they confounded the learned rabbis. The priests and the scribes, who were so deeply versed in the law, had nought to answer them.

These twelve unlettered fishermen, like twelve mighty conquerors, took counsel together and divided the whole world among themselves. They undertook to carry the word of the Lord to the uttermost ends of the earth.

They braved the fury of the Roman emperors, despised their threats and defied their tortures.

They confounded the philosophers of Greece and Rome, they penetrated into the remotest and most barbarous regions of the earth, triumphing wherever they went over the powers of darkness and corruption.

How did this come to pass, how did twelve poor men bring about such a mighty change?

Here is our lesson, here our consolation. They were weak and timid as we are—but aided by the grace and gifts given them by the Holy Spirit, nothing was impossible to them.

Holy writers tell us that the Holy Ghost came down on the Apostles more quickly and more abundantly because Mary was praying with them and for them.

Our prayer, when saying this Third Glorious Mystery, must be to implore God's holy Mother to obtain for us the plenitude of the strength and light of the Holy Spirit, His gifts, His graces in all their rich abundance, even as she did for the Apostles.

Many Christians live in lamentable ignorance of the invincible power of grace. They humbly confess their weaknesses and many miseries, but they almost despair of overcoming them. How foolish!

No matter how weak, how tempted we are, we can overcome every difficulty, with the help of God's grace and strength.

No saint, no apostle, no martyr did anything of himself, but they did the greatest things with God's grace.

This grace we shall get in abundance if we pray earnestly for it and if we receive the Sacraments devoutly and *frequently*.

The Sacraments are the great channels of grace between the Heart of God and our hearts.

We must not think that the Holy Ghost performed this marvelous transformation only in the case of the Apostles.

For three whole centuries, in the face of the fiercest persecutions, millions of martyrs, some young, weak and timid children, some old men and women, some gentle maidens, some men nurtured in luxury, became so strong, so brave, so fearless that they endured the most hideous and prolonged tortures, simply by the power they got from *grace*.

The Holy Spirit does the same for us. If, then, we are weak and sinful, the fault is all our own. We are trusting too much to our own strength, and we do not ask help from God.

The lesson on this mystery is that we can do nothing of ourselves — but everything with God's grace.

God's grace is a real force, a strength, a divine virtue, a power, a participation of the Divine Nature.

Many utterly fail to understand the nature and the power of grace.

Every time we say this Mystery, it must remind us to pray with all our hearts for **divine grace.**

A last thought. Every Catholic should practice devotion to the Holy Ghost. He, it is, who consoles and comforts us. He gives us light and faith to understand the truths of our religion.

Why are many Catholics so dull, so blind, so slow in comprehending the very greatest truths?

It is because they do not ask the Holy Ghost for faith and light, for comprehension and understanding of these truths.

They love and adore the Father and pray to Him most devoutly.

They honor God the Son made man, Our Lord Jesus Christ.

But many do not pray as much as they ought to pray to the Holy Ghost.

There are many beautiful prayers to the Holy Spirit. If we cannot find time to say one of these, let us at least say with special devotion the *Gloria Patri et Filio et Spiritui Sancto,* and also repeat with equal fervor the names of the Three Divine Persons, when we make the Sign of the Cross.

Chapter 30

THE ASSUMPTION

In this Fourth Glorious Mystery of the Rosary, we contemplate the most holy and happy death of our Blessed Lady and her glorious Assumption into Heaven.

God's Mother died a most holy death, she died of love. Her life had been so wonderful, so perfectly holy that her death was incomparably the holiest and happiest of any creature.

Our sweet Lord did not exempt even Himself from death—rather His death was the greatest proof of love that He gave us. So, too, He wished His dear Mother to die, that she might be like Him in all things.

He, however, conferred on her a second favor to manifest how much He loved her, how much He wished her to resemble Him.

She died a most holy death, and the Apostles placed her in a tomb. There that most blessed body remained for three days. The angels watched over it and sang heavenly canticles around it. Then it was assumed by God into Heaven, thus resembling most closely the glorious Resurrection of Christ from the dead.

Clearly, in this Mystery we must first of all thank God for the most holy and happy death He vouchsafed to His dear Mother.

Next, we must earnestly ask our Blessed Mother, by the holiness and happiness of her death, to obtain for us a happy death.

The moment of death decides our eternity. Infinite joy or infinite misery depends on our death. If this be holy and good, then we shall enjoy Heaven forever and ever. If our death be bad, our eternal lot will be cast with the devils in Hell.

Chapter 31

THE CORONATION OF OUR LADY IN HEAVEN

In this Mystery we contemplate the sublime glory of Mary in Heaven.

We love God's dear Mother. How could it be possible not to love one so gentle, so merciful, so sweet? She is loved by God Himself, she is His eldest daughter, His daughter above all others. He loved her more than all the rest of creation, for she is worthy of it. She is incomparably more holy, more beautiful, more gracious than all the angels and saints in Heaven. She is high above all creatures, and below God alone.

In the first moment of her existence she was dowered with more graces, more perfections than all other creatures. These graces were multiplied exceedingly every moment of her life. New and great graces were added, so that no human mind can comprehend the sanctity, the glory of Mary.

She has all virtues, all graces in the most eminent degree but, if we dare to say so, the grace that most attracts our poor human hearts to Mary is her sweetness, her clemency, her tender and gentle love for even the greatest sinners.

St. Bernard does not hesitate to say, and all the

Saints agree with him, that never was a sinner lost who called on Mary!

Never has it been known that she refused to hear a prayer that the least of us offer her.

There is another thought that we must not miss in this Mystery.

We love our sweet Mother, we go to her in all our troubles, in all our fears and doubts. We place unbounded confidence in her and, in truth, we can never place upon her too much.

We must not, however, be selfish. We must, in the first place, praise her and bless her with all our hearts; we must rejoice, we must exult at her great glory. She is not only our Mother, she is our Queen.

In this Mystery we consider her glory in Heaven. She is Queen where God is King.

The angels, burning with love, enraptured by the vision of her greatness and beauty, chant canticles of love and praise.

We, too, should praise our Queen, even as men who pour forth their cries of love and enthusiasm when their beloved sovereign passes in their midst.

We should exult and rejoice that God has made her His Mother, that He has made her Queen of Heaven. We should delight in honoring her privileges, her immaculate purity, her Divine maternity, her peerless beauty, her incomparable loveliness.

Therefore *the great thought* in this Mystery is to praise and exult in the glory of our Mother and our Queen.

She is Queen of Heaven. How little we know of Heaven, how little we think of Heaven—and because we do not think of Heaven, we lose the immense consolation such a thought would bring us.

If we only had some little idea of the happiness that awaits us, we should strive more earnestly to gain Heaven. How we should long for it!

One moment in Heaven will be sufficient reward for all the pains and sorrows of a hundred lives.

Let us remember, too, that every good act, every act of love will increase our merit in Heaven. An act of love that any of us can perform in a minute will have a reward, a recompense forever and ever in Heaven.

If we only thought of Heaven, it would console us in our bitterest sorrows. This is what St. Paul means when he says: "What are the sorrows and tribulations of this life in comparison with the glory that awaits us?"

We act like prisoners and slaves content with their miserable lot, who do not long for and sigh for their freedom. We are content with this vale of tears, this poor life with all its miseries, pains, and sorrows.

The happiness of Heaven should be our aim. It is perfect, complete, absolute. There we shall have no pains, no sorrows, nothing but infinite, immense, complete and perfect happiness. There all our desires shall be satisfied. Our joy will be full.

Mother of God, help us to understand what Heaven is.

It is lamentable that many Catholics seem to lose all the consolations, to miss all the beauty of our holy religion. Our religion is a religion of love, of peace, of happiness. Many fail to enjoy the wondrous love of God for them. They seem to have no idea of His friendship.

They may speak lovingly to Him in prayer, but instead, they make prayer a penance, a burden.

He dies for them really and truly every morning in the Mass. They do not seem to understand it; they certainly do not feel it.

Why not ask our sweet Mother to give us this foretaste of the joys of Heaven, which we should have in our holy religion?

Chapter 32

THE WONDERS OF HOLY MASS

The Saints never speak so eloquently as when they speak of the Mass. They can never say enough on this sublime subject, for, St. Bonaventure says the wonders of the Mass are as many as there are stars in the heavens and grains of sand on the seashores of the world.

The graces, blessings, and favors granted to those who assist at this Divine Sacrifice are beyond all comprehension.

The Mass is the greatest wonder in the world. There is nothing on earth equal to it, and there is nothing in Heaven greater than it.

The next greatest wonder is the indifference and ignorance of Catholics regarding Holy Mass. How is it that so many Catholics do not go to Mass?

The great Sacrifice of Calvary is offered near to their homes, almost at their very doors, and they are too slothful to assist at it.

The Sacrifice of Calvary! Yes, for the Mass is really and truly the very same as the death of Jesus on the Cross.

Why do not mothers, why do not catechists, why

164

do not teachers instill into the minds and hearts of those in their charge the wonders of the Mass? Priests are bound by the Council of Trent to do so.

Protestants may well ask those Catholics who neglect hearing daily Mass, *if they do really believe* that God is born on the altar, and that God dies on the altar as He did on Calvary? If they do believe, why do they not assist at Mass?

St. Augustine tells us that pagans and Gentiles of his time asked tepid and indifferent Christians with bitter irony if they sincerely believed that the God of all mercy and goodness descended on their altars! "You Christians," they continued, "accuse us of adoring false gods but, at least, we believe they are gods and we honor them, whereas you despise Him whom you call the True God!"

No intelligent, no enlightened Christian would fail to hear Mass if he only knew what it was.

ST. LOUIS AND THE MASS

King Louis of France, who labored perhaps more strenuously than any man in his kingdom and who was one of the best and most glorious sovereigns who ever ruled over France, found time to hear two or three Masses every day!

Some of his courtiers suggested that he was overtaking himself with so many Masses. The King replied: "If I spent much more time in following the pleasures of the chase, or in entertaining my friends at rich banquets, or in frequenting for several hours each day theaters and places of amusement, you would not complain that I was devoting too much time to pleasure.

"You forget, my good friends, that by hearing Mass I not only secure for myself innumerable blessings, but I confer the most important benefits on my kingdom, many more than I could possibly do in any other way."

This reply of St. Louis may be addressed to those thousands and thousands of apathetic and indifferent Christians who could easily hear daily Mass and do not do so.

Even were they to make a great sacrifice, they would receive blessings and favors above their highest hopes. But, as a matter of fact, many could hear Mass without any sacrifice, or at so trifling a cost that their guilt in neglecting this Divine Sacrifice is indeed incomprehensible. Nothing but lamentable ignorance can explain the reason why so many Catholics neglect to hear daily Mass.

By hearing Mass, the day would become worth a thousand days to them, so wonderful would be the graces and benefits they should receive.

Far from losing time, their business would prosper more and they would reach a degree of happiness that they could never otherwise hope to attain.

SIMON DE MONTFORT

The famous general and hero Simon de Montfort, with only 800 horse soldiers and very few foot soldiers, was unexpectedly trapped in the town of Muret by an army of 40,000 men, led by the King of Aragon and Raymond the Count of Toulouse. He was hearing Mass when his officers came to announce that the besieging army was marching to attack the town.

"Let me first finish Mass," he replied, "and then I will be with you."

He then hastened to where his forces were already gathered together, bade them trust in God, and ordering the gates to be flung open, he charged right at the heart of the approaching army, threw it into utter disorder, struck down the King of Aragon himself and won a glorious victory.

Baronius declares that the Emperor Lothaire heard three Masses every day, even when he was on the battlefield with his troops.

In the Great War it was well known that Marshall Foch, the Commander-in-chief of the French and British armies, heard Mass every day, even when the position was most critical.

The Emperor Otho of Germany once summoned a council of his chief officers and advisers, to take place in the Palace at Worms, at an early hour in the morning.

The Duke of Bohemia, one of the princes who was to take part in the Council, was wont to hear Mass daily and was, therefore, late in arriving at the Royal Palace.

This delay threw the Emperor into a fury, and without waiting for the Duke he commenced the Council, giving orders to all present not to show honor, or give any greeting to the Duke on his arrival.

Some short time after the Duke entered the Council chamber, and to the surprise of those present, the Emperor—who at first seemed startled — rose in haste and showed every mark of respect to the Duke. When the weighty matters of state had been discussed, the Emperor Otho, remarking the surprise manifested by the assembled lords and princes at his change of demeanor toward the Duke of Bohemia, explained: "Why," he said, "did you not see that he came accompanied by two angels, one on either side? I dared not show my resentment."

Similar wonderful favors are granted to the humblest of the faithful, to anyone who hears Mass devoutly.

Here are some incidents:

THE ANGEL AND THE ROSES

A poor farmer was wont to attend daily Mass for many years of his life.

He was crossing the snow-covered fields one cold morning on his way to church. He thought that he heard footsteps behind him, and turning he saw his angel guardian bearing a basket full of beautiful roses which exhaled a delicious perfume. "See," said the angel, "these roses represent each step you have taken on the way to Mass and each rose represents, too, a glorious reward which awaits you in Heaven. But far, far greater are the merits you have got from the Mass itself."

HOW TO MAKE ONE'S BUSINESS PROSPER

Two businessmen resided in the same French town. Both were engaged in the same line of commerce, but while one was prosperous, the other found it very hard to gain a sufficiency, notwithstanding that he worked harder and rose earlier than his friend.

Reduced to extremities, he resolved to seek advice from his prosperous colleague, hoping to learn the secret of his success.

"My good friend," replied the wealthy merchant, "I have no secrets, I work just as you work. If there is any difference in our methods it is this. I go to Mass daily. You do not. Follow my sincere advice, hear Mass every morning, and I feel sure that God will bless your work."

The poorer man did as he was advised and soon, in some unaccountable way, his difficulties ceased and his business prospered beyond all his expectations.

Chapter 33

WHAT IS THE MASS?

1. **In the Mass** the Son of God becomes man again, so that in every Mass the stupendous mystery of the Incarnation, with all its infinite merits, is repeated as truly as when the Son of God first took flesh in the womb of the Virgin Mary.

St. Augustine: "What a sublime dignity is that of the priest, in whose hands Christ once more becomes man."

2. **The Mass is the birth of Jesus Christ.** He is really born on the altar each time that Mass is said, as He was born in Bethlehem.

St. John Damascene: "If anyone wishes to know how the bread is changed into the Body of Jesus Christ I will tell him. The Holy Ghost overshadows the priest and acts on him as He acted on the Blessed Virgin Mary."

St. Bonaventure: "God, when He descends on the altar, does no less than He did when He became man the first time in the womb of the Virgin Mary."

3. **The Mass is the same as the Sacrifice of Calvary.** In it God dies as He died on the first

170

Good Friday. It has the same infinite value of Calvary and brings down on men the same priceless graces.

The Mass is not an imitation or a memory of Calvary, it is **identically the same Sacrifice** and differs only from Calvary in appearance.

In every Mass, the Blood of Jesus is shed for us again.

St. Augustine: "In the Mass, the Blood of Christ flows anew for sinners."

4. **Nothing on this earth,** nothing in Heaven itself, gives more glory to God and obtains more benefits for us than a single Mass.

5. **By the Mass we offer to God** the greatest praise, the greatest glory He could possibly desire. We give Him most perfect thanks for all the benefits He has bestowed on us. We make more reparation for our faults than by the severest penances.

6. **We can do nothing better** for the conversion of sinners than to offer for them the Holy Mass. If mothers would only hear and get Mass said for their erring children, and wives for their husbands, how happy should be their families!

7. **No prayers, no suffrages**—no matter how fervent—can help the Holy Souls as the Mass. Oh, let us think of the souls in Purgatory! Among them may be our dear father and mother and friends. We can help them most easily, we can relieve their

awful pains most efficaciously by hearing Mass for them.

WHAT THE SAINTS SAY OF THE MASS

To make still more manifest what we have just stated, we shall quote the very words of the Saints and Holy Doctors.

St. Laurence Justinian: "There is no prayer or good work so great, so pleasing to God, so useful to us as the Mass."

St. Alphonsus: "Even God Himself could do nothing holier, better, or greater than the Mass."

St. Thomas teaches that the Mass is nothing less than the Sacrifice of Calvary renewed on the altar, and every Mass brings to men the same benefits as the Sacrifice of the Cross.

St. Chrysostom: "The Mass has just the same value as Calvary."

St. Bonaventure: "The Mass is a compendium of all God's love, of all His benefits to men, and each Mass bestows on the world a benefit not less than what was conferred on it by the Incarnation."

St. Hanon, Bishop of Cologne, once saw a globe of extraordinary beauty and brilliancy circle round the Chalice at the Consecration and then enter the sacred vessel. He was so filled with awe that he feared to go on with the Mass, but God revealed to him that this happened at every Mass, though not visible to our human eyes.

The Host is nothing else than the great Eternal, Omnipotent God who fills Heaven with His Majesty. Why do not we realize it?

St. Odo of Cluny: "The happiness of the world comes from the Sacrifice of the Mass."

Timothy of Jerusalem: "The world would have been destroyed long ago because of the sins of men, had it not been for the Mass.

"There is nothing that appeases the anger of God so much, nothing that obtains for us so many blessings as the Mass."

St. Laurence Justinian: "No human tongue can describe the immense favors and blessings which we receive from the Mass. The sinner obtains pardon, the good man becomes more holy, our faults are corrected, and our vices uprooted by hearing Holy Mass."

Fornerius: "By one Mass which we hear in the state of grace, we give God more pleasure and obtain for ourselves more benefits and favors than by the longest and most painful pilgrimages."

Marchant: "If we were to offer to the Holy Trinity all the penances, all the prayers, all the good works of all the Saints, if we were to offer the torrents of blood, all the sufferings of the twelve Apostles and the millions of martyrs, all would give Him less glory and pleasure than one Mass! Why? Because the Mass is truly and really the Sacrifice of Mount Calvary. In the Mass, Jesus Christ offers to His Eternal Father all the pains, humiliations and infinite merits of His Passion and death."

The Mass obtains for us the very greatest graces, blessings, favors, spiritual and temporal, graces that we could not possibly receive in any other way.

It saves us from countless dangers and delivers us from the evils that threaten us.

St. Alphonsus asks, what is the reason of all this?

He answers that the Mass is infinite in value, whereas all the prayers and good works of the angels and saints, though of exceeding great merit, and though they give unspeakable glory to God, yet are finite, and therefore bear no comparison with the infinite Sacrifice of the Mass.

Just as all creation, the heavens and the earth, the sun, the moon and the stars, the mountains and oceans, all men and angels are nothing in comparison with God, so no good works, however holy, are equal to one Mass. The Mass is God Himself.

THE ANGELS AND THE MASS

St. Gregory: "The Heavens open, and multitudes of angels come to assist at the Holy Sacrifice."

St. Augustine: "The angels surround and help the priest when he is celebrating Mass."

St. John Chrysostom: "When Mass is being celebrated, the sanctuary is filled with countless angels, who adore the Divine Victim immolated on the altar."

The efficacy of the Mass is so wonderful, God's mercy and generosity are then so unlimited, that there is no moment so propitious in which to ask for favors as when Jesus is born on the altar. What we then ask we shall almost certainly receive, and what we do not obtain in the Mass we may scarcely hope to receive by all other prayers, penances or pilgrimages.

The angels know this full well and come in multitudes to adore God and make their petitions at this hour of mercy.

We read in the revelations of St. Bridget: "One day, when I was assisting at the Holy Sacrifice, I saw an immense number of holy angels descend and gather around the altar, contemplating the priest. They sang heavenly canticles that ravished my heart—Heaven itself seemed to be contemplating the great Sacrifice. And yet we poor, blind, and miserable creatures assist at the Mass with so little love, relish, and respect!

"Oh, if God would open our eyes, what wonders should we not see!"

When Bl. Henry Suso, the holy Dominican, was saying Mass, angels in visible form gathered round the altar, and some came near to him in raptures of love.

This is what takes place at every Mass, though we do not see it.

Do Catholics ever think of this amazing truth? At Mass they are praying in the midst of thousands of God's angels!

Chapter 34

THE JOY OF THE SAINTS AT MASS

St. Dominic was accustomed to pass the night in prayer before the Blessed Sacrament. In the morning he celebrated Mass with the fervor of a seraph, and was sometimes so filled with love and delight that his body was raised in the air and his face shone with a supernatural light.

St. John of the Cross said Mass with extraordinary love and devotion.

Once, having pronounced the words of Consecration, his face shone with such a brilliant light that many of those in the church gathered around the altar to gaze at the wonderful brightness.

After Mass the Superior begged him to say what had happened, and he replied: "At the Consecration, God revealed Himself to me in such majesty and glory that I feared that I could not continue the Mass."

Bl. John of Alverne said Mass with a like devotion. On the feast of the Assumption his soul was so filled with holy fear and emotion that he tried in vain to pronounce the words of Consecration. He began and paused, he began again and paused again. His superior, remarking his trouble, helped him to say the whole form.

Scarcely had Bl. John finished the words than he saw the Sacred Host take the form of the Divine Child—and he was so overcome that only with the help of two priests was he able to conclude the Holy Sacrifice.

He then fainted away in an ecstasy of love.

Thomas of Cantimbre, the celebrated Dominican Bishop who was famed for his profound learning and deep piety, describes a miracle which he himself witnessed in company with many others.

Having heard that Our Blessed Lord had appeared visibly in a Consecrated Host in the Church of St. Amand, in Douay, he hastened thither and begged the priest to open the Tabernacle and expose the sacred Particle. Many persons had flocked to the church on learning of the Bishop's arrival and were privileged to see once more Our Divine Lord.

The Bishop tells us what he himself saw: "I saw my Lord face to face. His eyes were clear and had an expression of wondrous love. His hair was abundant and floated on His shoulders. His beard was long, His forehead broad and high, His cheeks were pale and His head slightly inclined. At the sight of my loving Lord, my heart well nigh burst with joy and love.

"After a little time Our Lord's face assumed an expression of profound sadness, such as it must have worn in the Passion. He was crowned with thorns, and His Face was bathed in blood.

"On looking at the countenance of my sweet Saviour thus changed, my heart was pierced with bitter grief; tears flowed from my eyes, and I seemed to feel the points of the thorns enter my head."

St. John of the Augustinian Order was consumed with such a love for the Mass that he was accustomed to rise early in the morning in order to satisfy his eager desire to celebrate the Holy Sacrifice as soon as possible. His devotion was indeed admirable, and his soul was filled with rapture, especially at the moment of Consecration.

Those who served his Mass, however, complained to the superior that the good Father wearied them by the extraordinary length of time he took to say his Mass, which prevented them from fulfilling their other duties. The superior charged him to finish his Mass more speedily, like the other members of the community.

The good priest obeyed these instructions but, at the end of some days, he threw himself at the feet of the prior and implored him to be allowed to devote more time to the celebration of Holy Mass.

Urged by the superior to state his reasons for this unusual devotion, Fr. John revealed to him the divine favors he received, and how he visibly saw Jesus Christ on the altar, adding details that filled the prior with such great fear and emotions as almost made him faint.

The narration of these facts gave the superior a new and ardent fervor at Holy Mass during the remainder of his life.

St. Raymond of Penafort, Superior General of the Dominican Order, said Mass with angelic fervor. On one occasion a globe of fire covered his head and shoulders, like a glorious aureola, from the Consecration to the Communion of the Mass.

Bl. Francis of Possadas of the same Order was no less favored. His face shone with an extraordinary splendor and became beautiful in the extreme, as if he received new life. One day a flame of brilliant light issued from his mouth and lit up the missal when he was reading the Gospel. On two occasions during the feast of Pentecost a similar splendor emanated from his whole body and illuminated the altar.

When he was pronouncing the words of Consecration, Our Lord said to him with infinite love: "My son, I Am Who Am." After consuming the Host, his body was raised up and remained suspended in the air.

St. Ignatius was wont to say Mass with rapt devotion. One day the assistant saw a bright flame circle around his head and hastened to extinguish it, when lo, he discovered that it was a supernatural radiance that enveloped the head of the Saint!

Bl. Francis of the Order of Friars Minor suffered for many years from grievous pains in the legs so that any movement caused him intense suffering.

His devotion to the Mass was so great that during

all the years, full of faith, he arose from his couch in the morning and celebrated the Divine Mysteries without the slightest inconvenience.

Bl. John, a Dominican of Ravenna, was frequently seen enveloped in a heavenly splendor during Mass.

The lives of the Saints are full of similar marvels. What we must bear in mind, however, is that in every Mass we hear, no matter how humble the priest may be, the mysteries are the same, infinite in number, as St. Bonaventure says. It is the same Infinite, Omnipotent, Eternal God who is born on the altar and who offers Himself as truly as He did on Calvary, for those who assist at Mass.

Chapter 35

PRIESTS, THE HAPPIEST
OF MEN

Not only the Saints, but all devout priests experience the most profound satisfaction and joy when celebrating Mass.

It is enough for them to know:

1) That they are in immediate, intimate, personal communication with God Himself; that they are holding Him in their hands, looking at Him, conversing with Him, and that He is looking into their very hearts with ineffable love.

2) That they are giving Him the greatest possible joy and glory that even He could desire, greater glory than all the angels and saints give Him in Heaven.

3) That they are calling down on themselves, on the world, on their native land countless blessings.

4) That they are surrounded by throngs of holy angels who are watching their every movement.

5) Finally, that they are helping, consoling, rejoicing the Holy Souls in Purgatory.

How is it possible for a devout and intelligent priest to know and feel all this, and not be filled with joy.

THE MASS OF LEO XIII

"I was once admitted to assist at the Mass of Pope Leo XIII," a venerable priest told us, "and no book that I ever read on the Mass, no sermon I ever heard, produced on me such a profound impression.

"It is now fifty years since that happy day, and never since have I forgotten that Mass of the Holy Father. Never have I celebrated Mass myself that I have not tried to imitate the devotion he manifested at his Mass.

"The Pope was then 85 years of age, and seemed to me feeble, and considerably bent as he entered the chapel. When, however, he proceeded to the altar he was filled with a new life, a new energy.

"He began the Holy Sacrifice absorbed in devotion. All his gestures, all his movements, his slow, distinct utterance of the words showed clearly that he felt that he was in the very presence of God. At the moment of Consecration his face lit up with a beautiful light, his great eyes shone and his whole expression was as of one looking at, conversing with the Almighty.

"He took the Host in his hands with the utmost reverence and pronounced the solemn words of Consecration manifestly, with a full comprehension of the tremendous act he was performing.

"He then bent his knee as if before the throne of God in Heaven; he raised the Host aloft and gazed at It in rapture, slowly returning It to the corporal.

"He manifested the same unction and living faith at the Consecration of the most Precious Blood.

"Thence on to the Communion, his fervor was visible at every moment.

"At the *Agnus Dei* he seemed to be speaking face to face with God.

"I do not venture to describe with what love he consumed the Sacred Host and drank the Precious Blood of Jesus.

"And yet the Mass was not very long, the whole ceremony was simple but so impressive that, as I have said, it has been ever before my eyes for fifty long years."

A PROTESTANT CONVERTED BY THE MASS

A group of English tourists, Protestants, assisted at the Holy Sacrifice in the Cathedral Church of Florence. The celebrant said the Mass with deep devotion, quite unaware that he was being closely watched by this group of strangers. Some of the group, when their curiosity had been satisfied, left their places near the altar and proceeded to examine the beauties of the sacred edifice. One, however, remained behind and continued to watch every movement of the priest until the conclusion of the Holy Sacrifice.

He was evidently profoundly moved and was especially struck by the look of faith and joy visible on the priest's face as he came from the altar and proceeded to the sacristy. On his return to England, this gentleman begged for instruction and became a fervent Catholic.

We do not hesitate to say that when Protestants or unbelievers assist at a Mass said devoutly, they are frequently so deeply impressed that many of them, like the Englishman whom we have just mentioned, enter the Church.

HASTY AND IRREVERENT MASSES

Far different, says St. Alphonsus, are the sad results caused to those who assist at a Mass hastily and irreverently celebrated.

FR. MATEO CRAWLEY-BOEVEY

Fr. Mateo Crawley-Boevey was without doubt one of the greatest missionaries in the world. Yet there was no one more kind, more modest, more winning. Even when speaking of the greatest sinners, whom it had been his lot to encounter, he referred to them with kindness and pity.

Yet one fact he recounts with great sadness. We heard the story from his own lips. "My father," he said, "was a Protestant, a good living, honest, straightforward man. My mother was a Catholic and reared her children in the Catholic Faith. Her most ardent desire was to see my father converted. She acted with great tact and prudence. She placed her hope rather in prayer and example than in persuasion, though she found means, too, of making known to my father, without annoying him, the Truths of the Catholic Church.

"At last her hopes were on the verge of being fulfilled, so much so that my father promised to come with us to Mass.

"He did so, but unfortunately, the priest cele-

brated the Mass with so much haste and irreverence that my father returned home, disappointed and declared that never, never more,
would he think of becoming a Catholic.

"We, too, were profoundly disappointed, all the
more as my father refused to listen to any further
reference to the Catholic Faith. Years passed, and
we continued to pray.

"One evening a missionary priest of the Passionist Order called on us, and my father, in his
usual hospitable manner, invited him to remain.

"By a strange providence, the conversation of
this missionary produced a striking effect on my
father! Once more he consented to hear Mass, to be
celebrated by the missionary.

"The Passionist Father celebrated Mass very
simply, but very piously, and thanks to Almighty
God, my good father shortly after began a course of
instruction and entered the Church."

Chapter 36

THE BENEFITS OF THE MASS

St. Thomas, the prince of theologians, writes wonderfully of the Mass:

"The Mass," he says, "obtains for sinners in mortal sin the grace of repentance. For the just it obtains the remission of venial sins and the pardon of the pain due to sin. It obtains an increase of habitual grace, as well as all the graces necessary for their special needs."

St. Paul the Hermit stood once at the church door as the people entered. He saw the soul of one man, a great sinner, in such a state of horrible corruption as appalled him. Moreover, he saw a devil standing by his side who seemed to have complete control of him. On leaving the church, he saw the same man so completely changed that he called him aside and asked him confidentially if he was sorry for his sins. The poor man at once confessed that he had committed many and very grave sins, but during the Mass he had read in his prayer book: "If your sins are as red as scarlet I will make them as white as snow." "I began at once to ask God to pardon and forgive me, and I am very sorry for my sins and I wish to go to Confession at once."

St. Paul saw that by his act of sincere sorrow he was, by the infinite merits of the Mass, pardoned of all his sins.

Our Lord said to St. Mechtilde: "In Mass I come with such humility that there is no sinner, no matter how depraved he be, that I am not ready to receive if only he desires it. I come with such sweetness and mercy that I will pardon My greatest enemies if they ask for pardon. I come with such generosity that there is no one so poor that I will not fill him with the riches of My love. I come with such Heavenly Food as will strengthen the weakest, with such light as will illumine the blindest, with such a plenitude of graces as will remove all miseries, overcome all obstinacy and dissipate all fears."

What words of divine comfort, words of God Himself! If we heard nothing else about the Holy Mass, are not these words alone sufficient to fill us with faith and confidence in the Divine Mysteries?

St. Gregory of Nazianzen. In the life of this great saint we read that his father fell dangerously ill and was dying. The sick man had fallen into a state of such extreme weakness that he could scarcely make the slightest movement. His pulse was extremely weak, and he was not able to take any nourishment. At last he completely lost consciousness.

His family, despairing of all human means, placed their faith in God. They adjourned to the

church, where Mass was said for the recovery of
the sick man.

On their return, all danger had passed, and the
patient was soon perfectly restored to health.

The Holy Curé of Ars fell grievously ill, and
notwithstanding the constant help of doctors, grew
rapidly worse so that no hope was entertained of
his life.

He asked that a Mass be said on the Altar of St.
Philomena. At the conclusion of the Mass he was
completely cured.

In the city of Lisbon a lady lay dying of a mortal illness. The physicians held out no hope of
recovery. She was suffering from a malignant can-
cer, which had reached such extremes that an
operation was impossible.

Her confessor suggested that a Mass should be
offered for her complete cure.

The dying lady gladly accepted the counsel. The
Mass was offered in honor of St. Dominic, and by
its infinite efficacy the sick lady made a speedy
recovery, much to the joy of her friends and to the
surprise of her medical advisers.

How often do we not see in Christian homes the
parents, the brothers, or the sisters ill unto death.
Eminent physicians are summoned, costly remedies are purchased, no pains are spared to save the
dear ones from death and hasten their recovery.

All that is as it should be, but **why forget, why**

neglect the most potent of all remedies, the Holy Mass?

How many men and women who are now lying in their graves might be alive and well had Masses been offered for them as for the lady in Lisbon?

How many misfortunes and accidents would be avoided if men had faith and confidence in the infinite merits of the Holy Sacrifice?

If Catholics only understood the efficacy of the Mass, the churches would not be sufficient to hold the multitudes that would flock to assist at the celebration of the Divine Mysteries.

Would to God that Christian mothers assisted at and offered Masses for their families, and still better, if they trained their dear ones from their youth up to assist at Holy Mass.

THE MASS OBTAINS FOR US A HAPPY DEATH

The crowning grace of our life is a holy and happy death. What avails it to have had a long and happy life, to have enjoyed all the comforts which riches can give, all the honors the world can bestow, if in the end we die a bad death?

An unhappy death means a never-ending eternity of misery and woe.

We can only die **once,** and if we die badly there is no possibility of remedying the mistake. A bad death plunges a man into the fires of Hell forever and forever.

It is consequently of the utmost importance that we do all in our power, that we use every means to secure a happy death.

Holy writers recommend various excellent methods whereby we may make our salvation certain, and all these we should use to the best of our ability. All agree, however, that the best and easiest of these means is the frequent assistance at Holy Mass.

Our Blessed Lord assured St. Mechtilde that He would comfort and console all those who were assiduous in hearing Mass and that He would send as many of His great saints to assist them when dying as they had heard Masses in their lifetime.

Penellas relates that a devout man had such confidence in the efficacy of the Mass that he did his utmost to be present at the Holy Sacrifice as often as he possibly could.

He fell gravely ill and died with great peace and joy.

His parish priest grieved much at the loss of this exemplary member of his flock and offered for his soul many suffrages.

Great was the surprise of the good priest when the dead man appeared to him radiant with joy and thanked him for his charity, adding at the same time, that he was in no need of prayers, as owing to his frequent assistance at Mass he was received immediately into Heaven.

Msgr. Nautier, Bishop of Breslau, notwithstanding his onerous labors and grave responsibilities, sought to be present at as many Masses as he could which were celebrated in his cathedral.

At the moment of his death his soul was seen mounting up to Heaven, accompanied by many glorious angels who sang sweet canticles of joy and praise.

All good Christians would do well to follow these holy examples and ask God every time they hear Mass to grant them the grace of a holy death and freedom from the fires of Purgatory.

DO NOT MISS MASS

The obligation to hear Mass on Sundays and holydays is very grave, and to fail in the fulfillment of this duty on these days without sufficient reason is a mortal sin. Not only does the sinner thereby lose important graces which he may never again receive, but God may also punish him severely, as has frequently happened.

The following are some of the many instances we might mention:

The following fact happened near Rome. Three businessmen went to a fair at Cisterno, and after having transacted satisfactorily their business, two of them prepared to return home on Sunday morning. The third pointed out to them that they could not thus hear Mass. They laughed at his words and replied that they could go to Mass some other day. So saying, they mounted their horses and set out on their return journey.

Their companion heard Mass, and then proceeded

to follow them. What was not his consternation on learning that both his friends had been killed on the road, victims of a dreadful accident!

The writer of these lines remembers another awful punishment meted out by the Almighty to an unfortunate man in Rome itself. This man was a stone mason, and instead of hearing Mass on Sundays, he worked publicly, thereby giving no little scandal.

On the feast of Pentecost he was engaged as usual at his sinful work on a high scaffolding when, lo, he was precipitated to the ground and killed instantly!

St. Antoninus of Florence quotes another instance of untimely death as a penalty for not hearing Mass.

Two young men went off together to hunt. One had heard Mass, the other had not. A storm of thunder and lightning suddenly burst over them. One, the unfortunate man who had not gone to Mass, was struck dead by the lightning—whereas his companion escaped unscathed.

One of the principal duties of the Christian is to hear Mass on Sundays, the one day in the week consecrated to God. It is, indeed, very temerarious to neglect this obligation.

HOW A POOR BOY BECAME A BISHOP,
A CARDINAL AND A SAINT

Peter Damian lost both father and mother shortly after his birth. One of his brothers adopted him, but treated him with unnatural harshness, forcing him to work hard and giving him poor food and scanty clothing.

One day Peter found a silver piece, which represented to him a small fortune. A friend told him that he could conscientiously use it for himself, as the owner could not be found.

The only difficulty Peter had was to choose what it was he most needed, for he was in sore need of many things.

While turning the matter over in his young mind it struck him that he could do a still better thing—to have a Mass said for the Holy Souls in Purgatory, especially for the souls of his dear parents. At the cost of a great sacrifice, he put this thought into effect and had the Mass offered.

A complete change at once became noticeable in his fortunes.

His eldest brother called at the house where he lived, and horrified at the brutal hardships the little fellow was subjected to, arranged that he be handed over to his own care. He clad him and fed him as his own child, educated and cared for him most affectionately. Blessing followed on blessing. Peter's wonderful talents became known, and he was rapidly promoted to the priesthood; some time after, he was raised to the episcopacy and finally created Cardinal . . . Miracles attested his great sanctity so that after death he was canonized and made Doctor of the Church. These wonderful graces flowed, as from a fount, from that one Mass.

Chapter 37

PRIESTS, ANGELS ON EARTH

If we understand the divine dignity of the priesthood we shall comprehend more fully the infinite greatness of the Mass.

St. Ignatius Martyr says that the priesthood is the most sublime of all created dignities.

St. Ephrem calls it an infinite dignity.

Cassian says that the priest of God is exalted above all earthly sovereignties, and above all celestial heights—he is inferior to God alone.

Innocent the Third says that the priest is placed between God and man; inferior to God, but superior to man.

St. Denis calls the priest a divine man and the priesthood a divine dignity.

St. Ephrem says that the gift of the sacerdotal dignity surpasses all understanding.

Hence, **St. John Chrysostom** says that he who

honors a priest, honors Christ, and he who insults a priest, insults Christ.

St. Ambrose has called the priestly office a divine profession.

St. Francis de Sales, after having given orders to a holy ecclesiastic, perceived that in going out he stopped at the door as if to give precedence to another. Being asked by the Saint why he stopped, he replied that God favored him with the visible presence of his guardian angel, who before he had received the priesthood always remained on his right and preceded him, but now since the moment of Ordination, walked on his left and refused to go before him. It was in a holy contest with the angel that he stopped at the door.

According to **St. Thomas,** the dignity of the priesthood surpasses even that of the angels.

St. Gregory Nazianzen has said that the angels themselves venerate the priesthood.

All the angels in Heaven cannot absolve from a single sin. The guardian angels procure for the souls committed to their care, grace to have recourse to a priest, that he may absolve them.

St. Francis of Assisi used to say: "If I saw an angel and a priest, I would bend my knee first to the priest and then to the angel."

St. Augustine says that to pardon a sinner is a greater work than to create Heaven and earth.

To pardon a single sin requires all the omnipotence of God. See the power of the priest.

St. Alphonsus: "The entire Church cannot give God as much honor, or obtain so many graces as a single priest by celebrating a single Mass. Thus, by the celebration of a single Mass, in which he offers Jesus Christ in Sacrifice, a priest gives greater honor to the Lord than if all men, by dying for God, offered Him the sacrifice of their lives.

"With regard to the power of priests over the real Body of Jesus Christ, it is of faith that when they pronounce the words of Consecration, the Incarnate Word has obliged Himself to obey and to come into their hands under the sacramental species."

St. Ignatius Martyr: "Priests are the glory and the pillars of the Church, the doors and doorkeepers of Heaven."

St. Alphonsus: "Were the Redeemer to descend into a church and sit in a confessional, and a priest to sit in another confessional, Jesus would say over each penitent: *'Ego te absolvo.'* The priest would likewise say over each of his penitents: *'Ego te absolvo,'* and the penitents of each would be equally absolved. Thus the sacerdotal dignity is the most noble of all the dignities in this world."

St. Ambrose says that it transcends all the dignities of kings, of emperors, and of angels. The dignity of the priest as far exceeds that of kings as the value of gold surpasses that of lead.

St. Cyprian said that all who had the true spirit of God were, when compelled to take the Order of priesthood, seized with fear and trembling.

St. Epiphanius writes that he found no one willing to be ordained a priest, so fearful were they of so divine a dignity.

St. Gregory Nazianzen says in his *Life of St. Cyprian,* that when the Saint heard that his bishop intended to ordain him priest, he, through humility, concealed himself. It is related in the life of St. Fulgentius that he, too, fled away and hid himself.

St. Ambrose, as he himself attests, resisted for a long time before he consented to be ordained.

St. Francis of Assisi never consented to be ordained.

GOD REWARDS THOSE WHO HELP PRIESTS

A humble shopkeeper lived in a small town of Ireland with his wife and son. They had very little of this world's goods, but they were devout and went to Mass as often as they could.

A young priest, through ill health and overstudy, lost his mental balance and was unable to perform his priestly duties. He wandered from place to place, gentle and sweet, giving no one trouble.

The good shopkeeper proposed to his wife to give him a little room in their modest house and to give him food. The priest gladly accepted their kind invitation and spent some years with them, going and coming at his will.

Before death he regained the use of his reason, and sitting up in his dying bed, called on God most fervently to bless abundantly these good people: "Give them, dear Lord, a thousand fold for all they have given me, Your priest. Bless them spiritually and bless them temporally."

So saying, he died.

Wonderful to say, that modest shopkeeper grew in wealth and prosperity, so that his son became a millionaire and four of his sisters became nuns, and four of his wife's sisters became nuns. He himself lived to a ripe old age.

Those who contribute generously to the education of students for the priesthood receive great rewards, for they could not possibly do anything greater than offer a good priest to God.

No one on this earth can give God as much glory as a devout priest.

Chapter 38

HOW TO HEAR MASS WITH PROFIT

1) The first condition for hearing Mass well is to understand thoroughly the infinite sanctity of the Holy Sacrifice and the graces it obtains.

To this end we must read not once, but many times, this little book on the Mass.

The Mass, as we have seen, is a stupendous mystery. Our minds, on the other hand, are weak and slow to understand. Therefore, we must read frequently and ponder seriously on the wonders of the Mass. One Mass heard with understanding and devotion obtains for us more graces than a hundred, a thousand Masses heard carelessly and in ignorance of what the Mass is.

2) We should make it an inviolable rule to arrive at church some minutes before Mass commences, firstly, in order to be prepared and recollected when the priest comes on the altar, and, secondly, to avoid causing distraction to others.

3) We should not only hear Mass, but we should *offer* it with the priest. Moreover, we should have the intention of hearing and offering all the Masses being said at the same time all over the

world. In this way we receive a share in these innumerable Masses!

THE CROSS

4) We at once remark that the crucifix is on every altar, that the priest's vestments are all marked with the Sign of the Cross, that the priest commences the Mass with the Sign of the Cross, that he makes this holy sign very many times during the Mass. Why? To make clear to us that the Mass is really and truly the Sacrifice of the Cross, that in the Mass, Christ is crucified, sheds His Precious Blood and dies for us. We must have no doubt that **we are really assisting at the Sacrifice of the Cross.**

PRAYERS AT MASS

We must use any prayers that we wish and that help us most, but it is generally admitted that it is best to use a prayerbook and follow, as closely as we can, the Mass with the priest.

The Confiteor. When the priest bends down at the beginning of the Mass and says the Confiteor, we, too, should unite ourselves with Jesus in His agony, should humbly confess our faults and ask pardon for them through the merits of Christ's agony.

We then follow the various prayers with the celebrant.

At the Sanctus we should remember that the angels come down to assist at Mass in multitudes and that we are in the midst of them, and we should join our voices with theirs in adoring and praising God. They present our prayers to God.

At the Consecration we should be filled with the deepest reverence and love, for Jesus is really born in the hands of the priest, as He was born in Bethlehem. When the priest lifts up the Sacred Host, we should look on our God in an ecstasy of joy, as the angels look on Him in Heaven, and say: "My Lord and my God."

At the Consecration of the Precious Blood we must remember that all the Precious Blood that Jesus shed on Calvary is in the Chalice, and we should offer it to God with the priest for God's glory and for our own intentions.

It is well to place ourselves, our sorrow for our sins, all our intentions, our dear ones, the souls in Purgatory, in all the Chalices being at this moment offered to God in every part of the world.

We must be full of holy awe and love from the Consecration to the Communion. We are in the midst of countless adoring angels.

It is indeed a sign of woeful ignorance to manifest irreverence, to look around or speak during this most sacred time. It is much worse to leave the church, to abandon God dying on the altar for us. Nothing but the gravest necessity should induce one to go away until, at least, the Communion of the priest.

Remember, dear reader, that the day you hear Mass is worth a thousand days to you, that all the labors and works of a day, or a week or a whole year are nothing in comparison with the value of one Mass.

A WORD TO FATHERS AND MOTHERS

Reading these wonderful words of the Saints and Doctors of the Church, how is it possible that any Christian father or mother does not ardently desire to see at least one of their sons a priest.

Parents earnestly seek the welfare of their children, they strive to procure for them every happiness, every benefit, every honor.

How lamentable, then, is it that they so rarely seek for them the greatest of all honors, *viz.*, the priesthood.

It is true, we have heard of some families which count as many as three, four, six sons priests, but alas, these are very few!

Chapter 39

THE VALUE
OF SMALL THINGS

Many people are afraid of doing what is hard and difficult, but surely no one is so foolish and weak as to refuse to do what is easy and pleasant, when by doing so he can reap great and lasting benefits. No one hesitates to give a penny if in exchange he gets a pound; no one will refuse to dig a little in his garden if he is sure of finding there a great treasure.

Yet all of us have treasures within easy reach if only we know how and where to find them—and this is what we propose to tell our readers in the following pages.

Few Christians know the extraordinary value of small things.

Our Lord told St. Bridget and many others of His saints that our holiness and happiness consist in small things, even as the vast ocean consists of many little drops of water.

God may never ask us to do what is hard and heroic, but He does ask us *every day* to do countless simple and easy things. If we do these well—and nothing is easier—we shall soon attain to *great* holiness and also *great happiness*.

We shall now see:

First, the malice of **one bad thought or act** and what awful chastisements it deserves.

Secondly, the value of **one good act**—great, or small—and the eternal rewards it merits.

Thirdly, we shall point out a hundred little acts that we can perform every day with the greatest ease and pleasure, which will obtain for us unspeakably great rewards if only we do them as we ought to.

THE MALICE OF ONE BAD ACT

It was one act that plunged millions and millions of God's glorious angels into Hell for all eternity! One act!

It was one act, apparently very small, *viz.*, eating an apple, that has filled the world with sorrow and suffering for all these thousands of years and sent millions of men to Hell. Had Adam and Eve not eaten that apple, they and we—that is, all the human race—would never have suffered the smallest pain!

Remark well, dear reader, that the punishment with which God visited these sins was not in any way excessive. God could never punish sin too much, never more than the sin by its awful malice fully deserved. The punishment is what the malice of the sin demanded.

Therefore, we see what awful malice one small act can have in itself and what terrible chastisements it brings with it.

Someone may be inclined to think that these two

cases are exceptional. They are nothing of the kind.

Millions of men and women are every day committing mortal sins, and millions of men and women like ourselves are falling into Hell, just as the fallen angels did.

A mortal sin may be a bad thought, a word, or an act done in a moment. Yet it has in itself dreadful malice.

Venial sins, too, may be very grave, and because of their malice may be punished by long years in the fires of Purgatory.

Yet people commit so many venial sins every day. They shall have to give an account in the fires of Purgatory for *each* and *every* idle thought, word or act they may have committed, and they shall not leave these fires until they shall have paid the last farthing. These are the words of Our Lord Himself.

THE VALUE OF GOOD ACTS

On the other hand, let us clearly understand that as every evil act, great or small, is in itself vicious and brings us such dire chastisement, so *every good act* has in itself an immense value and will bring with it a corresponding weight of glory in Heaven.

The Good Thief on the cross had led a life of great crime and wickedness, and confessed that he richly deserved the awful death of crucifixion, yet by one short act of sorrow: "Lord, remember me when Thou comest into Thy Kingdom," he obtained full pardon for all his sins and merited to hear from Our Lord these wondrous words: *"This day wilt thou be with Me in Paradise."* Moreover, he became a saint and is known as St. Dismas.

The Poor Publican, weighed down with the heavy burden of many and grievous sins, was so conscious of his guilt that he dared not approach the holy part of the Temple, but fell on his knees, struck his breast, bowed his head and said these few words: "God, have pity on me, a sinner."

By this simple act he received complete pardon for all his sins!

The Widow's Mite. One day Our Blessed Lord was in the Temple on a feast day, and the princes of the people and the great and wealthy Jews came and cast rich alms into the treasury of the Temple. At last a poor widow came and cast her mite, all she could afford, into the alms-box. Our Lord, who observed all that had passed, turned to His Apostles and said: "That poor woman has given more than all the rest."

It is not the act—it is the intention of the giver that gives value to the action.

Again, one may say that these are exceptional cases, but we answer, by no means. Similar rewards are being given every day for like small acts.

Any alms we give, no matter how small, and no matter to whom it is given, for love of God, will have a reward just as if we gave it to God Himself!

This He makes most abundantly clear, for He says: "When the good shall appear before Me, I will say to them: Come, ye blessed of My Father, take possession of the Kingdom prepared for you, for when I was hungry you gave Me to eat, when I was thirsty you gave Me to drink, when I was naked you clothed Me.

"And they will answer: But Lord, we never had the happiness of seeing You, of giving You to eat, or to drink, or of clothing You. I will reply: Every time you gave it to the least of My little ones, you gave it to Me.

"I will say to the wicked: Begone, ye accursed of My Father, for when I was hungry you gave Me not to eat, when thirsty you gave Me not to drink, when naked you did not clothe Me. And they will say: But Lord, we never saw You on earth, we never refused to give You to eat, to give You to drink, to clothe You. And I will say: Each time you refused it to the least of My poor, you refused it to Me. Begone from Me forever."

Even if we give a **cup of cold water** to a poor man in God's name, we shall have an eternal reward. That, too, is Christ's promise.

These promises are amply verified in the lives of the Saints, for many times when they gave alms to the poor, Our Lord revealed to them that He considered the alms as given to Himself.

St. Martin, when a soldier and not yet a Christian, once gave half his military cloak to a poor man, as he had nothing else with him at the moment to give. That night Our Lord appeared to him clad in the cloak and said: "Martin the Catechumen gave Me this cloak."

Bl. Jordan of Saxony, a student in the University of Bologne, was once accosted by a beggar who asked him to give him something for the love of God. Jordan, who had nothing else at the moment to give, took off a most valuable girdle encrusted with precious stones which he wore, and gave it to the mendicant. A few moments after he entered a church, and to his amazement, saw his girdle buckled around the waist of the figure of Christ on the Cross!

Jordan became a great saint, the successor of St. Dominic as General of the Dominican Order, and one of the most zealous apostles of his time.

John Gualbert, a Florentine nobleman, pardoned a man who had murdered his brother because the murderer asked him to do so for the love of Jesus. Entering a church immediately afterwards, he knelt at the feet of the crucifix. Our Lord looked at him with infinite sweetness and bowed His head most lovingly toward him. John, filled with divine grace, became a saint and a founder of a religious Order.

St. Anthony of the desert, when still a rich young man in the world, once heard a sermon with great attention. As a result of that sermon he became not only a saint, but the father and model of saints.

St. Ignatius became a saint by reading one good book.

Blessed Imelda became a saint by one Holy Communion.

Peter Damian, a poor boy, once found a silver coin, and not being able to discover its owner, asked the parish priest to say Mass for his intention. This was indeed, a brave act, the poor boy needed many things.

So pleased was God with this act that Peter became a bishop, a cardinal, a saint and Doctor of the Church.

So we, too, can gain immense rewards by doing small things. Let us see how.

Chapter 40

EJACULATIONS

We exhort you, dear reader, to read with the closest attention this chapter on ejaculations. Nothing is easier, nothing more useful and profitable to us than these little prayers, which we can say at every moment. Nothing will make us more happy.

The custom of making short ejaculatory prayers is one of the surest ways of becoming both holy and happy. So far from being irksome, it fills our hearts and souls with a profound peace and joy.

There are hundreds of moments in the day when we can, without difficulty, make these short, fervent, spontaneous prayers which shoot up from our hearts to the throne of God in Heaven and bring down on us showers of graces and blessings.

These ejaculations should be made lovingly and joyfully, just as if we were speaking face to face to Our Lord—as indeed we are—for He hears even the smallest prayer or sigh we send up to Him.

THE FIRST MOMENTS OF THE DAY

When we arise in the morning, the devil tries to snatch the *first fruits* of the day from God. Many foolish Christians lose these precious moments.

211

The devil, ever on the watch to do us harm, fills our minds with useless, sad, futile thoughts, and strange—unthinking Christians never open their eyes to this deplorable fact.

These first moments of the morning are perhaps the most valuable in the whole day because, if we use them as every Christian should do, we secure for ourselves a happy day and the certain protection and blessing of God. They deliver us, too, from a thousand dangers and evils.

We take twenty minutes, or half an hour, perhaps, to wash and dress. What are we thinking of during these most precious minutes? We often-times think of something sad and disagreeable, something that happened yesterday, or else we are worrying about something that we have to do today; our minds are filled with some trouble or annoyance that molests or threatens us. These moments are far from cheerful, far from holy, full of little worries.

Instead, they should be full of joy and confidence in God. He has given us a new day. When little birds wake, they shake their wings and pour forth their joyous song of praise to their Maker. Surely we can do as much as these tiny songsters. All the time that we are washing and dressing we should be pouring forth little prayers, chatting, as it were, with our sweet Lord, who is, as we have said, lis-tening to us and loving us.

There need be no effort. The prayers should flow spontaneously from our hearts.

Is there any difficulty in saying them? None

whatever. On the contrary, they fill us with new life and energy, and they banish those sad and depressing thoughts which make so many lives miserable.

During the day we can continue them *countless times,* when walking, or working, or riding in cars, at home, or in the streets, when changing our clothes to go out, or after coming in, when waiting for anyone, but especially, when inclined to be sad or cast down, when in fear of any difficulty, or anxious to obtain any favor.

There are busy men and women who are saying ejaculations hundreds and hundreds of times in the day. Why do not we do so? One day that we make ejaculations may get us more graces than we otherwise should get in a whole year.

There are very many beautiful ejaculations, but we recommend more especially three for frequent use.

"JESUS, JESUS, JESUS"

The first of these is the shortest and most efficacious of all. It consists of one short word, **Jesus.** This we may repeat as often as we like. We have to add nothing, only repeat the one word, **Jesus.**

It is St. Paul who recommends it in a most striking way.

He tells us that each time we pronounce the word **Jesus**: 1) We give the utmost joy and glory to the Eternal Father, to Mary the Mother of Jesus, to all the angels and Saints in Heaven! 2) Every time we say it we receive most copious graces and benedictions. 3) We drive the devil from our sides. 4) We protect ourselves from all kinds of evils.

He advises us to do everything we do in the name of Jesus.

Each time we say this one word, we make an act of most perfect love and say a prayer so powerful that God cannot resist it, as Our Lord Himself told His Apostles and the multitudes who surrounded Him: **"Everything you ask the Father in My name you shall receive."** What a promise! God cannot deceive us, God cannot give us a promise which He does not fulfill, God never exaggerates.

Moreover, we gain, each time we pronounce the Holy Name of Jesus, 300 days indulgence,* which we may offer for the Holy Souls. What hundreds of souls can we not thus take out of Purgatory, and these will be our greatest friends in Heaven.

WHY IS THE NAME OF JESUS SO POWERFUL?

The meaning of **Jesus** is God-made-man. Every time we say this Name, we offer to God the Incarnation, Passion and death of Jesus Christ. We offer Him all the Masses being said all over the world, for the Mass is Jesus born on the altar and dying on the altar as He died on Calvary. We do not offer a mere name; each time we say **Jesus**, we offer God all the infinite merits of Jesus Christ.

---

* Indulgences are now designated simply as *plenary* or *partial*.

PROOFS OF THE POWER OF THE HOLY NAME

The Apostles worked all their miracles and converted the world with the Name of Jesus.

St. Paul loved the Name of Jesus most ardently. He wrote it more than two hundred times in his Epistles, not from necessity, but impelled by the purest love.

A crippled man asked St. Peter for an alms. The great Apostle lovingly answered: "Gold and silver I have none, but what I have, I willingly give you: 'In the **Name of Jesus** get up and walk.'" In an instant the man leaped up and walked, to the amazement of all present.

After the example of Sts. Peter and Paul, the Apostles and all the Saints have ever cherished the greatest faith and confidence in the Name of Jesus and have worked the most astounding miracles simply by this one word: **Jesus.**

St. Augustine tells us that he never cared for books if they did not speak of Jesus. The name of Jesus gave him immense delight.

St. Bernard says: "The Name of Jesus is like honey in my mouth. It fills my soul with peace and joy and love."

St. Dominic and **St. Francis** of Assisi were filled with joy when they pronounced the **Name of Jesus,** because they thought at once of all the love, the sweetness and the mercy of Jesus.

St. Francis de Sales experienced intense pleasure in repeating this Name. He says: "Oh, how happy we shall be when dying if we have had the custom of constantly saying, 'Jesus, Jesus, Jesus,' during our lives!"

St. Leonard used to preach on the Holy Name with such fervor that tears came to the eyes of his listeners. He recommended them to constantly repeat it, to paint it on their doors, for it would preserve their homes from sickness and sorrow.

Once a Jew refused to allow a Christian who lived with him to paint it on his door, so that the Christian had to be content to paint it on his windows.

Some time after, a fire broke out in the house and utterly destroyed everything, until it reached the windows which had the Name of Jesus painted on them. Here it stopped and went no further.

All the Saints loved to repeat the Name of Jesus, and placed their confidence in it.

Let us do likewise and we too shall enjoy the powerful protection of Jesus.

The following facts give ample proof of the irresistible power of the Holy Name.

The Count of Armogasto, one of the principal lords in the court of Genseric, the King of the Vandals, refused to change his faith as the King wished him to do.

The barbarian, incensed at this refusal, ordered the Count to be tortured most brutally—but in vain—for the martyr stood firm.

As a final effort, his executioners bound him tightly with the strongest cords, causing him excruciating pain.

He simply repeated the name of Jesus a few times, and the cords snapped as spiders' webs.

The torture was renewed, and this time the cords used were made of the sinews of oxen and were sunk deep into the Count's flesh by the brute force used to tighten them. Again the martyr repeated, "Jesus, Jesus, Jesus," and the sinews snapped and fell in pieces at his feet.

He was next bound by the feet, swung into the air and left hanging, head downwards. Once more he repeated, "Jesus, Jesus, Jesus," and at once fell into a sweet and tranquil sleep, as though reclining on the softest bed.

In the year 1861, D. Melchior, a Dominican Bishop, was martyred in China in circumstances of the most appalling savagery.

After having undergone many terrible sufferings he was stripped of his garments and surrounded by five brawny executioners, each armed with a hatchet having teeth like a saw. With these they began to hew the Bishop to pieces bit by bit. First they hacked off one leg slowly, piece by piece, with twelve dreadful blows, then the other leg, then one arm, then the second, then his flesh. After this they tore out his intestines with fiendish cruelty and finally smashed his head in pieces.

During this indescribable and prolonged torture, the Bishop kept on repeating with the utmost calm and serenity: "Jesus, Jesus, Jesus."

Not even once in his awful agonies did he cry

out, or groan, or even show by any contraction of his face the extremity of his pains, so that all who looked on were lost in amazement.

DEVOTION TO THE NAME OF JESUS IN PORTUGAL

We might add many other equally striking examples of the divine power of the Name of Jesus, but we content ourselves with one more fact, which served to establish love and confidence in the Holy Name in a *whole country* for several centuries!

During the reign of the famous King John I of Portugal, a virulent plague broke out all over the country of Portugal. It raged with the utmost fury in the city of Lisbon.

Thousands and thousands of men, women and children were swept off. Men rose in the morning and were dead before night. Some died at table when eating their meals, some died in the streets. Priests, doctors and infirmarians died in such numbers that few were left to attend to the dying or bury the dead. Those who died in the streets lay unburied. The dogs lapped up their blood and ate their flesh. These, too, were seized with the pest and died. The air was reeking with corruption, and all hope seemed lost. Those who could fly from the city did so in thousands.

Amongst the most arduous helpers of the sick was Frei André Dias, a Dominican bishop, then resident in Lisbon. He labored all day and late into the night. Nothing could abate his zeal.

But even he lost hope in human aid when he saw that the plague was ever on the increase. Instead, therefore, he placed his trust in the Name of Jesus, to which he was very devout.

He went around the streets, entered the houses, spoke with unexampled faith and confidence of the power of the Name of Jesus. He inflamed the hearts not only of those who were well, but of the sick and the dying with love and trust in the Holy Name. He told the people to say constantly, **"Jesus, Jesus, Jesus."**

He bade them write it on cards and carry these in their pockets, nail them on their doors and in every room of their houses. When he had filled their sorrowing hearts with faith and confidence in the Name of Jesus, he called on all to come to the great Church of Saint Dominic. There he said solemn Mass in honor of the Name of Jesus and preached with a burning eloquence, never heard before, on the power of this most Holy Name. He blessed a great quantity of water in the Name of Jesus and told the people to sprinkle with it those who were sick, to dip their handkerchiefs in the water and bathe the foreheads of those dying in the streets and to carry it to their homes. He solemnly promised them that if they called on the Name of Jesus with faith and if they used this blessed water, Jesus in His infinite mercy would deliver them from the awful plague.

They did as he commanded, and in a few days the pest completely disappeared!

Great then was the love and trust awakened in the hearts of the people for the blessed Name of the Saviour.

The news of this astounding miracle spread throughout the length and breadth of the country. All the people of Portugal called on the Name of Jesus, used the blessed water, painted the Holy Name on their doors and in their rooms as had been done in Lisbon, and in an incredibly short time the whole country was delivered from one of the most dreadful chastisements it had ever experienced.

For long centuries this burning love for the Holy Name continued in all Portugal.

Only in 1834, when the religious Orders as well as many other good priests were expelled, did this glorious devotion almost fade from the memory of the Portuguese people.

THE NAME OF JESUS IN AMERICA

God in His mercy, however, raised up a new apostle in the United States of America, a Dominican, where the grand old devotion of Portugal was, as it were, transplanted and took firm root.

Very soon the association of the Holy Name spread through every part of the great American republic. The Bishops themselves, seeing the wonderful results wrought by it, became each in his own diocese, the head or president of the association to which, because of its extraordinary importance, the Holy Father gave a special Cardinal Protector whose duty it is to stimulate, conjointly with the Bishops, love and confidence in the Name of Jesus.

The American government, though in the main Protestant, looks on this famous association as a bulwark of American life and order, so much so that the President of the United States, though a Protestant, attends the annual reunion in person and gives unstinted praise to the magnificent work done by the Holy Name Society.

So powerful and energetic is this society that it has more than two million members, men of every age and profession, lawyers, doctors, professors, workmen, sailors, soldiers and policemen. When America entered the Great War and the President called for conscripts, no less than 500,000 members of the Holy Name sodality joined the army.

No soldiers gave proof of more heroic courage, simply because they were filled with the true spirit of patriotism and their lives were so pure that death had no fears for them.

The great resolution that we beg every reader of these pages to make is the resolution proposed to us by St. Paul and by all the Saints, *viz.,* to repeat constantly every day of our lives, in all troubles, fears, doubts and difficulties—*hundreds of times every day*—**"Jesus, Jesus, Jesus."** If we do so we shall surely become holy, and become happy.

To pronounce *once* the name of **Jesus** is a perfect act of love, an irresistible prayer. What then will it be if we say it hundreds and hundreds of times every day? Dear reader, you have here the secret of immense happiness in your hands.

The second ejaculation we recommend is:

"O SACRED HEART OF JESUS,
I PLACE MY TRUST IN THEE!"

These few words repeated frequently during the day place us under the immediate and personal protection of Our Lord. We are in His hands; no evil can harm us.

Firstly, He revealed to St. Gertrude that those who say this little prayer fill His Sacred Heart with joy! What a consolation for anyone to know that He fills the Heart of Jesus with pleasure!

Secondly, He gives them, *each time* they say it, a special and a great grace.

Thirdly, they gain each time 300 days indulgence,* which they can give to the Souls in Purgatory.

In recent years He spoke to that most privileged and holy soul, Benigna Consolata, and told her that by repeating these words we give Him the greatest possible pleasure in our power!

There is no better way of practicing devotion to His Sacred Heart than by repeating this little prayer frequently.

We can, by practice, repeat it hundreds and hundreds of times in the day, and it ought to be our intention to say it with the love and confidence of the Blessed Mother of God herself. Then, indeed, it becomes of immense value.

The third ejaculation which we recommend is:

---

* See footnote p. 214.

"JESUS, MARY, JOSEPH"

This short prayer is so powerful that, whereas the Church grants 300 days indulgence to other ejaculations, it grants 3,000 days to this one.*

Each time we say these three words 1) We place ourselves under the protection of Jesus, Mary, and Joseph. 2) We ask Jesus, Mary, and Joseph to deliver us from all evils and sins. 3) We ask them for all the beautiful virtues of peace, prudence and gladness which they practiced in Nazareth. 4) We ask them most especially for the grace of a happy death.

As in the case of the others, we should strive to say this short and most efficacious prayer every moment of the day. Nothing we can do is calculated to obtain for us greater peace and happiness.

OTHER EJACULATIONS

We have recommended these ejaculations more especially as they are short and easy and are more commonly in use. But there are many other beautiful ejaculations which we can also say with the greatest utility.

"THY WILL BE DONE"

This short prayer we say every time we recite the Our Father, and we should lay special stress on the words.

No act is so important as to do the Will of God. Every time we do the Will of God, whether in small

---

* See footnote p. 214.

things or in great, we are doing the most perfect thing we can possibly do.

St. Francis de Sales says that to wish to do the Will of God is of unspeakable merit.

He lays down the following teaching, which must fill the coldest heart with comfort. He says that if an ordinary Christian learns from the priest or the doctor that he is dying, and that if he accepts death with resignation because it is God's Will, he may go straight to Heaven. Why? Because death is the penalty God gave us for sin. It is the greatest of all penalties, the destruction of our life, the rending apart of the body from the soul—and at the same time it is the holiest and most meritorious of all penances.

Pope Pius X seems to have had this teaching in mind when he granted a plenary indulgence at the hour of death to those who say, on some day after receiving Communion, this short prayer: **"O my God, from this moment forward I accept with a joyful and resigned heart the death You will be pleased to send me, with all its pains, sufferings and anguish."**

Though the Holy Father grants a plenary indulgence if this prayer be said **once,** still it is advisable to say it after **every** Holy Communion. It takes only a moment and is of great merit.

Neither should we be satisfied with saying the words: **"Thy will be done"** only when we say the Our Father; we should do well to say them as an ejaculatory prayer very often in the course of the day.

We should wish to do the Will of God in everything we do. It would be madness not to do so, because God's Will is the very best thing for us. This we have already said when treating of the Our Father, but we can never impress it too deeply on our hearts.

"JESUS, MEEK AND HUMBLE OF HEART, MAKE MY HEART LIKE UNTO THINE"

This short prayer will most certainly obtain for us two great virtues, the most necessary of all virtues for our daily lives: humility and patience.

Humility is completely misunderstood by a vast number of Christians. They think that it is a painful and disagreeable virtue, a virtue repugnant to human nature. This is the gravest error anyone could make. It is the most beautiful of virtues and the one that makes us thoroughly and profoundly happy. God loves the humble—He can refuse them nothing. He resists the proud and refuses them everything.

When we say the words: **"Jesus, meek and humble of heart, make our hearts like unto Thine,"** we ask Our Lord to make us like Himself, to make us sweet and gentle like His own dear Mother. No one was so lovable as Jesus was, no one so sweet as Mary.

When we say these words, we should have the intention of offering the Eternal Father the infinite humility, meekness, and patience of His Divine Son and of asking Him by the merits of Our Lord to make us patient and humble.

Impatience and irritability are the ruin of our

lives. There is no virtue so absolutely necessary in our daily life as patience.

Consequently we should strive to repeat very often this most useful ejaculation: "Jesus, meek and humble of heart, make my heart like unto Thine."

"THE WORD WAS MADE FLESH AND DWELT AMONGST US"

Our Lord revealed to St. Gertrude that this short prayer gives Him such immense joy that when a devout Christian repeats it, He then turns to His Eternal Father and offers the infinite merits of His Incarnation for that person.

Who will not frequently repeat this wonderful prayer, sure of obtaining such a reward?

O Jesus, by Thy Passion and death, in union with all the Masses now being said, deliver us from all evils and sin.

O Jesus, wash us in Thy precious Blood.

Blessed be the most Holy and Immaculate Conception of the Blessed Virgin Mary, Mother of God.

O Mary, conceived without sin, pray for us who have recourse to thee.

These two ejaculations give the Mother of God great pleasure and obtain for us many graces, especially the virtue of purity.

O St. Joseph, for the love of Jesus and Mary, hear our prayers and obtain our petitions.

St. Philomena, for the love of Jesus and Mary, help us.

St. Philomena, the Wonder Worker, as the Popes call her, is working the most astounding wonders every day, curing the sick, helping those in trouble, comforting her clients. The day one begins to know this dear little saint is one of the happiest days of one's life, as a venerable priest used to say.

Chapter 41

WHAT THE SAINTS SAY
OF EJACULATIONS

The custom of making ejaculations is of such transcendent importance that all the Saints practiced it and raised themselves to an eminent height of sanctity by its means. They urge us to follow their example—so easy and simple—and assure us that we, too, shall receive the greatest graces.

The reasons they give are manifest:

1) Nothing is easier; the weakest and most timid of men can make ejaculations.

2) We lose no time, because we make these little ejaculations in the hundreds of free moments we all have during the day, or even at night when we cannot sleep.

3) Every ejaculation, no matter how short, can be an act of perfect love, a most efficacious prayer.

For example, the shortest of all prayers, the one word, **"Jesus,"** is so powerful that God cannot resist it; it may and often has worked great miracles.

4) Every ejaculation gives great pleasure to God, obtains great graces for us, and by reason of the indulgences attached to it, gives relief to the

souls in Purgatory.

5) By ejaculations we keep ourselves ever in the presence of God, we secure His protection and obey the command of Our Lord to "Pray always."

6) These ejaculations obtain for us the profoundest consolations. They are most particularly useful to the sick, who have to pass long hours lying down, unable to work or amuse themselves.

7) Above all, they secure for us a holy and a happy death.

From this we see that ejaculatory prayer is of the most vital importance.

THE DIFFICULTY IN MAKING EJACULATIONS

The difficulty in making ejaculations is that the devil, who well knows the glory that we give to God and the innumerable graces that we shall ourselves receive by their means, will do all in his power to prevent our saying them—he will try to make us relax our efforts.

Therefore, we should spare no pains to acquire the custom of saying them every day and many times in the day.

To help us to remember them we should, at the end of our morning prayers, renew our resolve to make them without fail during the day, and at night ask ourselves how many times we have made them.

No sacrifice is too great for the acquiring of this habit.

Once acquired we shall find our hearts full, full of joy and consolation.

WHEN CAN WE SAY EJACULATIONS?

Always. Hundreds of times in the day. When dressing in the morning, when working, when waiting for anything, at home, in the streets, when walking or driving, especially when sad and troubled.

One day that we say these ejaculations has the value of a thousand days.

Far from tiring us, they fill us with peace, joy and happiness.

Chapter 42

OUR ANGEL GUARDIANS

It is, indeed, an act of base ingratitude to neglect and ignore our dear guardian angel as so many do.

We must always have before our eyes the fact that God's holy angel is ever at our side, day and night, since the moment we were born. Never once has he taken his eyes off us.

We must remember that our angel is one of the princes of Heaven, that he loves us most tenderly and is ever protecting us from countless dangers that we do not even see.

He is ever pleading with God for us, obtaining for us immense helps and graces. He is as really by our side as someone who is walking with us. All his love and attention are for us.

And yet how many never even think of this glorious, loving, bright, mighty angel. They never say a prayer to him, they never once thank him. He is their best friend, he is powerful and loving, yet they never ask his help.

The writer once asked a venerable bishop with whom he was traveling in a motor car through a crowded city if he was afraid of accidents, as a little time before, some serious collisions had taken place.

"Oh, no!" he replied. "When I get into a motor car I at once place myself under the care of my guardian angel: that is sufficient."

Another friend made a similar reply: "When traveling, especially in crowded thoroughfares, I promise to offer the first Mass I hear, in honor of my angel, and I am sure of his help."

HOW CAN WE HONOR OUR ANGELS?

We should accustom ourselves, first of all, to call on him in every trouble, fear or pain, whether great or small.

We must not only call on him in great things, but in *every* trouble.

After our morning offering we should speak to our dear angel most familiarly. He is standing by our side looking at us, smiling on us. We must ask him to help us, to protect us during the day, to deliver us from all troubles and dangers.

In the course of the day we should do well to call on him constantly, lovingly; nothing will give him more joy. We should frequently offer our Masses, our Communions in his honor.

How is it that Christian mothers do not instill deeply and clearly and *constantly* into the minds of their dear children what a powerful, loving, affectionate friend they always have near them, in the dark hours of night and at every moment during the day.

The thought of our guardian angel should be like the thought of our dear mother herself. He is as present to us as she is, he loves us even more. What an immense consolation!

It is above all when we are young that we should be convinced that our angel is ever near us to defend us, to help us, to get us everything good. Yet we scarcely ever hear children speaking of, or calling on their angels. They hear a great deal of nonsense about ghosts, which impresses them deeply, but little about their glorious angels.

Few children ever think of the presence and protection of their dear angels, because this grand and all-important truth was never impressed on them, and then later on, as men and women, they utterly ignore their angels. How sad!

Catechists and teaching sisters do not attach anything like due importance to this most consoling and helpful doctrine of the Church.

What is more lovely, more beautiful, more full of interest than that we have glorious angels, princes of Heaven, watching over us, loving us, ever by our sides, as really as our brothers and sisters, but oh, infinitely more loving and infinitely more helpful!

How many men long for friends in whom they can place all their confidence, friends who love them, friends who can and will console and help them. And yet they have the dearest, best, most loving of all friends always with them—and they never speak to him, never even think of him!

This is an incomprehensible lack of instruction on one of the most consoling doctrines of the Church.

But if we have not learned about our angels

when young, let us, in God's name, do so at once. Let us have, as we ought, a vivid feeling of their presence by our sides; let us love them, pray to them and trust them.

PRAYER TO OUR ANGELS

My God, I thank Thee for all the graces Thou hast given to my dear angel.

My God, I thank Thee for having given me this great angel to be my brother and my friend.

My dear angel, I thank thee thousands and thousands of times for the countless favors thou hast done me, for the countless times thou hast saved me from evils and dangers.

My angel, I love thee with all my heart. Make me feel thy presence at my side.